Visit Cram101.com for full Practice Exams

Visit Cram101.com for full Practice Exams

Textbook Outlines, Highlights, and Practice Quizzes

Understanding Western Society: A Brief History Vol. 1

by John P. McKay, 1st Edition

All "Just the Facts101" Material Written or Prepared by Cram101 Publishing

Title Page

Visit Cram101.com for full Practice Exams

WHY STOP HERE... THERE'S MORE ONLINE

With technology and experience, we've developed tools that make studying easier and efficient. Like this Craml0l textbook notebook, **Craml0l.com** offers you the highlights from every chapter of your actual textbook. However, unlike this notebook, **Craml0l.com** gives you practice tests for each of the chapters. You also get access to in-depth reference material for writing essays and papers.

By purchasing this book, you get 50% off the normal subscription free!. Just enter the promotional code **'DK73DW21995'** on the Cram101.com registration screen.

CRAMI0I.COM FEATURES:

Outlines & Highlights
Just like the ones in this notebook, but with links to additional information.

Integrated Note Taking
Add your class notes to the Cram101 notes, print them and maximize your study time.

Problem Solving
Step-by-step walk throughs for math, stats and other disciplines.

Practice Exams
Five different test taking formats for every chapter.

Easy Access
Study any of your books, on any computer, anywhere.

Unlimited Textbooks
All the features above for virtually all your textbooks, just add them to your account at no additional cost.

Be sure to use the promo code above when registering on Craml0l.com to get 50% off your membership fees.

STUDYING MADE EASY

This Craml0l notebook is designed to make studying easier and increase your comprehension of the textbook material. Instead of starting with a blank notebook and trying to write down everything discussed in class lectures, you can use this Craml0l textbook notebook and annotate your notes along with the lecture.

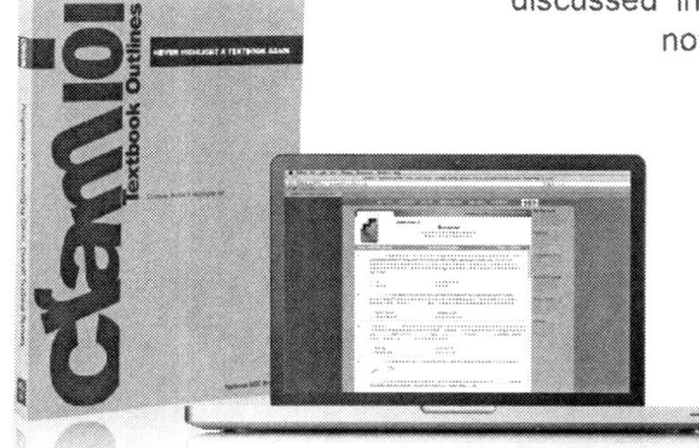

Our goal is to give you the best tools for success.

For a supreme understanding of the course, pair your notebook with our online tools. Should you decide you prefer Craml0l.com as your study tool,

we'd like to offer you a trade...

Our Trade In program is a simple way for us to keep our promise and provide you the best studying tools, regardless of where you purchased your Craml0l textbook notebook. As long as your notebook is in *Like New Condition**, you can send it back to us and we will immediately give you a Craml0l.com account free for 120 days!

Let The* Trade In *Begin!

THREE SIMPLE STEPS TO TRADE:

1. Go to www.cram101.com/tradein and fill out the packing slip information.
2. Submit and print the packing slip and mail it in with your Craml0l textbook notebook.
3. Activate your account after you receive your email confirmation.

* Books must be returned in *Like New Condition*, meaning there is no damage to the book including, but not limited to; ripped or torn pages, markings or writing on pages, or folded / creased pages. Upon receiving the book, Craml0l will inspect it and reserves the right to terminate your free Craml0l.com account and return your textbook notebook at the owners expense.

"Just the Facts101" is a Cram101 publication and tool designed to give you all the facts from your textbooks. Visit Cram101.com for the full practice test for each of your chapters for virtually any of your textbooks.

Cram101 has built custom study tools specific to your textbook. We provide all of the factual testable information and unlike traditional study guides, we will never send you back to your textbook for more information.

YOU WILL NEVER HAVE TO HIGHLIGHT A BOOK AGAIN!

Cram101 StudyGuides

All of the information in this StudyGuide is written specifically for your textbook. We include the key terms, places, people, and concepts... the information you can expect on your next exam!

Want to take a practice test?

Throughout each chapter of this StudyGuide you will find links to cram101.com where you can select specific chapters to take a complete test on, or you can subscribe and get practice tests for up to 12 of your textbooks, along with other exclusive cram101.com tools like problem solving labs and reference libraries.

Cram101.com

Only cram101.com gives you the outlines, highlights, and PRACTICE TESTS specific to your textbook. Cram101.com is an online application where you'll discover study tools designed to make the most of your limited study time.

By purchasing this book, you get 50% off the normal monthly subscription fee!. Just enter the promotional code **'DK73DW21995'** on the Cram101.com registration screen.

www.Cram101.com

Copyright © 2013 by Cram101, Inc. All rights reserved.
"Just the FACTS101"®, "Cram101"® and "Never Highlight a Book Again!"® are registered trademarks of Cram101, Inc.
ISBN(s): 9781478493334. PUBX-3.201388

Understanding Western Society: A Brief History Vol. 1
John P. McKay, 1st

CONTENTS

1. Origins, ca. 400,000-1100B.C.E.

CHAPTER OUTLINE: KEY TERMS, PEOPLE, PLACES, CONCEPTS

- Western world
- Jehovah
- Neolithic
- Mesopotamia
- Cradle of civilization
- Ideogram
- City-state
- Epic of Gilgamesh
- Sumer
- Society
- Ziggurat
- Amorite
- Babylon
- Geography of Egypt
- Atlantic slave trade
- Novel
- Akhenaten
- Hittites
- Hattusa
- Battle of Kadesh
- Neo-Babylonian Empire

Visit Cram101.com for full Practice Exams

1. Origins, ca. 400,000-1100B.C.E.

CHAPTER OUTLINE: KEY TERMS, PEOPLE, PLACES, CONCEPTS

Sea Peoples

Anatolia

CHAPTER HIGHLIGHTS & NOTES: KEY TERMS, PEOPLE, PLACES, CONCEPTS

Western world

The Western world, is a term referring to different nations depending on the context. There is no agreed upon definition about what all these nations have in common.

The concept of the Western part of the earth has its roots in Greco-Roman civilization in Europe, with the advent of Christianity.

Jehovah

Jehovah is the romanization of Hebrew ???????, a vocalization of the Tetragrammaton ???? (YHWH, also transcribed Yahweh), the proper name of the god of Israel in the Hebrew Bible.

??????? appears 6,518 times in the traditional Masoretic Text, in addition to 305 instances of

Neolithic

The Neolithic Era, or Period, from ν?ος (néos, 'new') and λ?θος (líthos, 'stone'), or New Stone age, was a period in the development of human technology, beginning about 10,200 BC, according to the ASPRO chronology in some parts of the Middle East, and later in other parts of the world and ending between 4,500 and 2,000 BC.

Traditionally considered the last part of the Stone Age, the Neolithic followed the terminal Holocene Epipaleolithic period and commenced with the beginning of farming, which produced the 'Neolithic Revolution'. It ended when metal tools became widespread (in the Copper Age or Bronze Age; or, in some geographical regions, in the Iron Age). The Neolithic is a progression of behavioral and cultural characteristics and changes, including the use of wild and domestic crops and of domesticated animals.

Mesopotamia

Mesopotamia (from the Ancient Greek: : '[land] between rivers'; Arabic: ? (bilad al-rafidayn); Syriac: (Beth Nahrin): 'land of rivers') is a name for the area of the Tigris-Euphrates river system, corresponding to modern-day Iraq, the northeastern section of Syria and to a lesser extent southeastern Turkey and smaller parts of southwestern Iran.

Widely considered to be the cradle of civilization in the West, Bronze Age Mesopotamia included Sumer and the Akkadian, Babylonian, and Assyrian empires, all native to the territory of modern-day Iraq. In the Iron Age, it was controlled by the Neo-Assyrian and Neo-Babylonian empires.

Cradle of civilization

The cradle of civilization is a term referring to any of the possible locations for the emergence of civilization. It is usually applied to the Ancient Near Eastern Chalcolithic (Ubaid period, Naqada culture), especially in the Fertile Crescent (Levant and Mesopotamia), but also extended to sites in Armenia, and the Persian Plateau, besides other Asian cultures situated along large river valleys, notably the Indus River in the Indian Subcontinent and the Yellow River in China.

Civilization is usually taken to presuppose the presence of agriculture and urban settlements, and as such is a consequence of the Neolithic Revolution.

Ideogram

An ideogram is a graphic symbol that represents an idea or concept. Some ideograms are comprehensible only by familiarity with prior convention; others convey their meaning through pictorial resemblance to a physical object, and thus may also be referred to as pictograms.
Terminology

The term 'ideogram' is commonly used to describe logograms in writing systems such as Egyptian hieroglyphs, Sumerian cuneiform and Chinese characters.

City-state

A city-state is an independent or autonomous entity whose territory consists of a city which is not administered as a part of another local government. A city-state can also be defined as a central city and its surrounding villages, which together follow the same law, have one form of government, and share languages, religious beliefs, and ways of life. Today, only three independent, sovereign city-states exist: Monaco, Singapore, and Vatican City.

Epic of Gilgamesh

The Epic of Gilgamesh is an epic poem from Mesopotamia and is among the earliest known works of literature. Scholars believe that it originated as a series of Sumerian legends and poems about the protagonist of the story, Gilgamesh king of Uruk, which were fashioned into a longer Akkadian epic much later. The most complete version existing today is preserved on 12 clay tablets from the library collection of 7th-century BC Assyrian king Ashurbanipal.

Sumer

Sumer was an ancient civilization and historical region in southern Mesopotamia, modern Iraq, during the Chalcolithic and Early Bronze Age. Although the earliest historical records in the region do not go back much further than ca. 2900 BC, modern historians have asserted that Sumer was first settled between ca. 4500 and 4000 BC by a non-Semitic people who may or may not have spoken the Sumerian language (pointing to the names of cities, rivers, basic occupations, etc. as evidence).

1. Origins, ca. 400,000-1100B.C.E.

CHAPTER HIGHLIGHTS & NOTES: KEY TERMS, PEOPLE, PLACES, CONCEPTS

Society

A society, is a group of people related to each other through persistent relations, or a large social grouping sharing the same geographical or virtual territory, subject to the same political authority and dominant cultural expectations. Human societies are characterized by patterns of relationships (social relations) between individuals who share a distinctive culture and institutions; a given society may be described as the sum total of such relationships among its constituent members. In the social sciences, a larger society often evinces stratification and/or dominance patterns in subgroups.

Ziggurat

Ziggurats (, Akkadian ziqqurat, D-stem of zaqaru 'to build on a raised area') were massive structures built in the ancient Mesopotamian valley and western Iranian plateau, having the form of a terraced step pyramid of successively receding stories or levels.

Notable ziggurats include the Great Ziggurat of Ur near Nasiriyah, Iraq; the Ziggurat of Aqar Quf near Baghdad, Iraq; Chogha Zanbil in Khuzestan, Iran; and Sialk near Kashan, Iran. Description

Ziggurats were built by the Sumerians, Babylonians, Elamites, Akkadians, and Assyrians for local religions.

Amorite

Amorite refers to an ancient Semitic-speaking people who occupied large parts of Mesopotamia from the 21st Century BC. The term Amurru in Akkadian and Sumerian texts refers to them, as well as to their principal deity.

Origin

In the earliest Sumerian sources, beginning about 2400 BC, the land of the Amorites ('the Mar.tu land') is associated not with Mesopotamia but with the West, including what is now modern Syria and Canaan. They appear as nomadic people in the Mesopotamian sources, and they are especially connected with the mountainous region of Jebel Bishri in Syria called the 'mountain of the Amorites'.

Babylon

Babylon occurs in the Christian New Testament both with a literal and a figurative meaning. The famous ancient city, located near Baghdad, was a complete unpopulated ruin by 275 BC, well before the time of the New Testament. In the Book of Revelation, the city of Babylon seems to be the symbol of every kind of evil

Geography of Egypt

The Geography of Egypt relates to two regions: Southwest Asia and North Africa.

Egypt has coastlines on both the Mediterranean Sea and the Red Sea. The country borders Libya to the west, the Gaza Strip and Israel to the east, and Sudan to the south.

Atlantic slave trade

The Atlantic slave trade or trans-atlantic slave trade took place across the Atlantic ocean from the 16th through to the 19th centuries. The vast majority of slaves transported to the New World were Africans from the central and western parts of the continent, sold by Africans to European slave traders who then transported them to the colonies in North and South America. The numbers were so great that Africans who came by way of the slave trade became the most numerous Old-World immigrants in both North and South America before the late eighteenth century. The South Atlantic economic system centered on making goods and clothing to sell in Europe and increasing the numbers of African slaves brought to the New World.

Novel

A novel is a long prose narrative that describes fictional characters and events in the form of a sequential story, usually. The genre has historical roots in the fields of medieval and early modern romance and in the tradition of the novella. The latter, an Italian word used to describe short stories, supplied the present generic English term in the 18th century.

Akhenaten

Akhenaten known before the fifth year of his reign as Amenhotep IV, was a Pharaoh of the Eighteenth dynasty of Egypt who ruled for 17 years and died perhaps in 1336 BC or 1334 BC. He is especially noted for abandoning traditional Egyptian polytheism and introducing worship centered on the Aten, which is sometimes described as monotheistic or henotheistic. An early inscription likens the Aten to the sun as compared to stars, and later official language avoids calling the Aten a god, giving the solar deity a status above mere gods.

Akhenaten tried to bring about a departure from traditional religion, yet in the end it would not be accepted.

Hittites

The Hittites were an Ancient Anatolian people who established an empire at Hattusa in north-central Anatolia around the 18th century BC. This empire reached its height during the mid-14th century BC under Suppiluliuma I, when it encompassed an area that included most of Asia Minor as well as parts of the northern Levant and Upper Mesopotamia. After c. 1180 BC, the empire came to an end during the Bronze Age collapse, splintering into several independent 'Neo-Hittite' city-states, some of which survived until the 8th century BC.

The Hittite language was a member of the Anatolian branch of the Indo-European language family. They referred to their native land as Hatti, and to their language as Nesili (the language of Nesa).

Hattusa

Hattusa was the capital of the Hittite Empire in the late Bronze Age. It was located near modern Bogazkale, Turkey, within the great loop of the Kizil River. Hattusa was added to the UNESCO World Heritage list in 1986.

Battle of Kadesh

The Battle of Kadesh took place between the forces of the Egyptian Empire under Ramesses II and the Hittite Empire under Muwatalli II at the city of Kadesh on the Orontes River, in what is now the Syrian Arab Republic.

The battle is generally dated to 1274 BC, and is the earliest battle in recorded history for which details of tactics and formations are known. It was probably the largest chariot battle ever fought, involving perhaps 5,000-6,000 chariots.

Neo-Babylonian Empire

The Neo-Babylonian Empire or the Chaldean Empire was a period of Mesopotamian history which began in 626 BC and ended in 539 BC. During the preceding three centuries, Babylonia had been ruled by their fellow Akkadian speakers and northern neighbours, Assyria. Throughout that time Babylonia enjoyed a prominent status. The Assyrians had managed to maintain Babylonian loyalty through the Neo-Assyrian period, whether through granting of increased privileges, or militarily, but that finally changed in 627 BC with the death of the last strong Assyrian ruler, Assurbanipal, and Babylonia rebelled under Nabopolassar the Chaldean the following year.

Sea Peoples

The Sea Peoples, were a confederacy of seafaring raiders from Southern Europe, especially the Aegean Sea who sailed around the eastern Mediterranean and invaded Anatolia, Syria, Canaan, Cyprus, and Egypt toward the end of the Bronze Age.

The Sea Peoples are documented during the late 19th dynasty and especially during year 8 of Ramesses III of the 20th Dynasty when they tried to enter or control the Egyptian territory. The Egyptian Pharaoh Merneptah explicitly refers to them by the term 'the foreign-countries of the sea' (Egyptian) in his Great Karnak Inscription.

Anatolia

32°E? / ?39°N 32°E? / 39; 32

Anatolia (from Greek ?νατολ? Anatole -- 'east' or '(sun)rise'; also Asia Minor, from Greek: Μικρ? ? σ?α Mikrá Asía 'small Asia'; in modern Turkish: Anadolu) is a geographic and historical term denoting the westernmost protrusion of Asia, comprising the majority of the Republic of Turkey. The region is bounded by the Black Sea to the north, Georgia to the northeast, the Armenian Highland to the east, Mesopotamia to the southeast, the Mediterranean Sea to the south and the Aegean Sea to the west. Anatolia has been home to many civilizations throughout history, such as the Hittites, Phrygians, Lydians, Persians, Greeks, Assyrians, Armenians, Romans, Byzantines, Anatolian Seljuks and Ottomans.

1. An _________ is a graphic symbol that represents an idea or concept. Some _________s are comprehensible only by familiarity with prior convention; others convey their meaning through pictorial resemblance to a physical object, and thus may also be referred to as pictograms. Terminology

   The term '_________' is commonly used to describe logograms in writing systems such as Egyptian hieroglyphs, Sumerian cuneiform and Chinese characters.

   a. IMFI
   b. Inherent vowel
   c. International Movement Writing Alphabet
   d. Ideogram

2. _________ known before the fifth year of his reign as Amenhotep IV, was a Pharaoh of the Eighteenth dynasty of Egypt who ruled for 17 years and died perhaps in 1336 BC or 1334 BC. He is especially noted for abandoning traditional Egyptian polytheism and introducing worship centered on the Aten, which is sometimes described as monotheistic or henotheistic. An early inscription likens the Aten to the sun as compared to stars, and later official language avoids calling the Aten a god, giving the solar deity a status above mere gods.

   _________ tried to bring about a departure from traditional religion, yet in the end it would not be accepted.

   a. Alashiya
   b. Amarna art
   c. Amarna Period
   d. Akhenaten

3. The _________ Era, or Period, from ν?ος (néos, 'new') and λ?θος (líthos, 'stone'), or New Stone age, was a period in the development of human technology, beginning about 10,200 BC, according to the ASPRO chronology in some parts of the Middle East, and later in other parts of the world and ending between 4,500 and 2,000 BC.

   Traditionally considered the last part of the Stone Age, the _________ followed the terminal Holocene Epipaleolithic period and commenced with the beginning of farming, which produced the '_________ Revolution'. It ended when metal tools became widespread (in the Copper Age or Bronze Age; or, in some geographical regions, in the Iron Age). The _________ is a progression of behavioral and cultural characteristics and changes, including the use of wild and domestic crops and of domesticated animals.

   a. Pollen zone
   b. Preboreal
   c. Shigir Idol
   d. Neolithic

4. . _________s (, Akkadian ziqqurat, D-stem of zaqaru 'to build on a raised area') were massive structures built in the ancient Mesopotamian valley and western Iranian plateau, having the form of a terraced step pyramid of successively receding stories or levels.

Notable _________s include the Great _________ of Ur near Nasiriyah, Iraq; the _________ of Aqar Quf near Baghdad, Iraq; Chogha Zanbil in Khuzestan, Iran; and Sialk near Kashan, Iran. Description

_________s were built by the Sumerians, Babylonians, Elamites, Akkadians, and Assyrians for local religions.

a. Second Servile War
b. Viking Age
c. Baptism of Poland
d. Ziggurat

5. The _________ or the Chaldean Empire was a period of Mesopotamian history which began in 626 BC and ended in 539 BC. During the preceding three centuries, Babylonia had been ruled by their fellow Akkadian speakers and northern neighbours, Assyria. Throughout that time Babylonia enjoyed a prominent status. The Assyrians had managed to maintain Babylonian loyalty through the Neo-Assyrian period, whether through granting of increased privileges, or militarily, but that finally changed in 627 BC with the death of the last strong Assyrian ruler, Assurbanipal, and Babylonia rebelled under Nabopolassar the Chaldean the following year.

a. Pumbedita
b. Sura
c. Tammuz
d. Neo-Babylonian Empire

Visit Cram101.com for full Practice Exams

ANSWER KEY
1. Origins, ca. 400,000-1100B.C.E.

---

1. d
2. d
3. d
4. d
5. d

You can take the complete Chapter Practice Test

for 1. Origins, ca. 400,000-1100B.C.E.
on all key terms, persons, places, and concepts.

Online 99 Cents

http://www.epub141.56.21995.1.cram101.com/

Use www.Cram101.com for all your study needs

including Cram101's online interactive problem solving labs in

chemistry, statistics, mathematics, and more.

2. Small Kingdoms and Mighty Empires in the Near East, ca. 1100-513B.C.E

CHAPTER OUTLINE: KEY TERMS, PEOPLE, PLACES, CONCEPTS

- Anatolia
- Mesopotamia
- Novel
- Kingdom of Kush
- Phoenicia
- Sidon
- Amorite
- Exodus
- Golden calf
- Passover
- Ten Commandments
- Jerusalem
- Ark of the Covenant
- Palestine
- Neo-Babylonian Empire
- Bactria
- Achaemenid Empire
- Last Judgment

2. Small Kingdoms and Mighty Empires in the Near East, ca. 1100-513B.C.E.

Anatolia	32°E? / ?39°N 32°E? / 39; 32 Anatolia (from Greek ?νατολ? Anatole -- 'east' or '(sun)rise'; also Asia Minor, from Greek: Μικρ? ?σ?α Mikrá Asía 'small Asia'; in modern Turkish: Anadolu) is a geographic and historical term denoting the westernmost protrusion of Asia, comprising the majority of the Republic of Turkey. The region is bounded by the Black Sea to the north, Georgia to the northeast, the Armenian Highland to the east, Mesopotamia to the southeast, the Mediterranean Sea to the south and the Aegean Sea to the west. Anatolia has been home to many civilizations throughout history, such as the Hittites, Phrygians, Lydians, Persians, Greeks, Assyrians, Armenians, Romans, Byzantines, Anatolian Seljuks and Ottomans.
Mesopotamia	Mesopotamia (from the Ancient Greek: : '[land] between rivers'; Arabic: ? (bilad al-rafidayn); Syriac: (Beth Nahrin): 'land of rivers') is a name for the area of the Tigris-Euphrates river system, corresponding to modern-day Iraq, the northeastern section of Syria and to a lesser extent southeastern Turkey and smaller parts of southwestern Iran. Widely considered to be the cradle of civilization in the West, Bronze Age Mesopotamia included Sumer and the Akkadian, Babylonian, and Assyrian empires, all native to the territory of modern-day Iraq. In the Iron Age, it was controlled by the Neo-Assyrian and Neo-Babylonian empires.
Novel	A novel is a long prose narrative that describes fictional characters and events in the form of a sequential story, usually. The genre has historical roots in the fields of medieval and early modern romance and in the tradition of the novella. The latter, an Italian word used to describe short stories, supplied the present generic English term in the 18th century.
Kingdom of Kush	The Kingdom of Kush, White Nile and River Atbara in what is now the Republic of Sudan. Established after the Bronze Age collapse and the disintegration of the New Kingdom of Egypt, it was centered at Napata in its early phase. After king Kashta ('the Kushite') invaded Egypt in the 8th century BC, the Kushite kings ruled as Pharaohs of the Twenty-fifth dynasty of Egypt for a century, until they were expelled by Psamtik I in 656 BC. During Classical Antiquity, the Kushite imperial capital was at Meroe
Phoenicia	Phoenicia was an ancient Semitic civilization situated on the western, coastal part of the Fertile Crescent and centered on the coastline of modern Lebanon. All major Phoenician cities were on the coastline of the Mediterranean, some colonies reaching the Western Mediterranean. It was an enterprising maritime trading culture that spread across the Mediterranean from 1550 BC to 300 BC. The Phoenicians used the galley, a man-powered sailing vessel, and are credited with the invention of the bireme.
Sidon	35°23′53″E? / ?33.56056°N 35.39806°E? / 33.56056; 35.39806

Visit Cram101.com for full Practice Exams

Sidon,or Saïda, is the third-largest city in Lebanon. It is located in the South Governorate of Lebanon, on the Mediterranean coast, about 40 km (25 mi) north of Tyre and 40 km (25 mi) south of the capital Beirut. Its name means a fishery.

Amorite

Amorite refers to an ancient Semitic-speaking people who occupied large parts of Mesopotamia from the 21st Century BC. The term Amurru in Akkadian and Sumerian texts refers to them, as well as to their principal deity.

Origin

In the earliest Sumerian sources, beginning about 2400 BC, the land of the Amorites ('the Mar.tu land') is associated not with Mesopotamia but with the West, including what is now modern Syria and Canaan. They appear as nomadic people in the Mesopotamian sources, and they are especially connected with the mountainous region of Jebel Bishri in Syria called the 'mountain of the Amorites'.

Exodus

Exodus is a video game that was released for the Nintendo Entertainment System by Color Dreams through its Wisdom Tree label in 1991. Like all Wisdom Tree games, Exodus was not officially licensed by Nintendo.

According to the game's instruction manual, the player controls the biblical figure Moses as he leads the Israelites to the promised land, meaning he goes through a labyrinth. Moses has the ability to shoot glowing 'W's, which signify the word of God, to defeat enemies and remove obstacles.

Golden calf

According to the Hebrew Bible, the golden calf was an idol (a cult image) made by Aaron to satisfy the Israelites during Moses' absence, when he went up to mount Sinai. In Hebrew, the incident is known as ?e?' ha'eggel or 'The Sin of the Calf'. It is first mentioned in Exodus 32:4.

Passover

Christian Passover is a religious observance celebrated by some churches to keep faith with Old Testament teaching. It is often linked to the Christian holiday and festival of Easter. Often, only an abbreviated seder is celebrated to explain the meaning in a time-limited ceremony.

Ten Commandments

The Ten Commandments, is a list of religious and moral imperatives that, according to the Hebrew Bible, were given by God to the people of Israel from the mountain referred to as Mount Sinai or Horeb. The Bible describes their form as being spoken by God and subsequently as an inscription on two stone tablets which God wrote with his finger, after which God gave the tablets to Moses. The Ten Commandments are recognized as a moral foundation in Judaism and Christianity.

2. Small Kingdoms and Mighty Empires in the Near East, ca. 1100-513B.C.E.

CHAPTER HIGHLIGHTS & NOTES: KEY TERMS, PEOPLE, PLACES, CONCEPTS

Jerusalem	Jerusalem or On Religious Power and Judaism (original: „Jerusalem oder über religiöse Macht und Judentum') is the title of a book written by Moses Mendelssohn, which was first published in 1783 - the same year, when the Prussian officer Christian Wilhelm von Dohm published the second part of his Mémoire Concerning the amelioration of the civil status of the Jews. Moses Mendelssohn was one of the key figures of Jewish Enlightenment (Haskalah) and his philosophical treatise, dealing with social contract and political theory (especially concerning the question of the separation between religion and state), can be regarded as his most important contribution to Haskalah. The book which was written in Prussia on the eve of the French Revolution, consisted of two parts and each one was paged separately.
Ark of the Covenant	The Ark of the Covenant is a biblical vessel, described in (1 Kings 8:9) as solely containing the Tablets of Stone on which the Ten Commandments were inscribed. According to Hebrews 9:4 and some traditional interpretations of Exodus 16:33-34 and Numbers 17:25-26, the Ark also contained Aaron's rod and a jar of manna. The ark is a symbol of God's permanent covenant(s) with the Jewish people and others who believe in accord with the Judaic scriptures (Christianity, Islam, etc)..
Palestine	Palestine ; Arabic: ??????? Filas?in, Falas?in, Filis?in) was a conventional name, among others, used between 450BCE and 1948AD to describe a geographic region between the Mediterranean Sea and the Jordan River, and various adjoining lands. The boundaries of the region have changed throughout history, and were first defined in modern times by the Franco-British boundary agreement (1920) and the Transjordan memorandum during the British Mandate for Palestine. Today, the region comprises the country of Israel and the Palestinian territories.
Neo-Babylonian Empire	The Neo-Babylonian Empire or the Chaldean Empire was a period of Mesopotamian history which began in 626 BC and ended in 539 BC. During the preceding three centuries, Babylonia had been ruled by their fellow Akkadian speakers and northern neighbours, Assyria. Throughout that time Babylonia enjoyed a prominent status. The Assyrians had managed to maintain Babylonian loyalty through the Neo-Assyrian period, whether through granting of increased privileges, or militarily, but that finally changed in 627 BC with the death of the last strong Assyrian ruler, Assurbanipal, and Babylonia rebelled under Nabopolassar the Chaldean the following year.
Bactria	Bactria, later variously Tukharistan, Tokharistan, and Tocharistan, was the ancient name of a historical region in Central Asia, located between the range of the Hindu Kush and the Amu Darya (Oxus). It was a part of the northeastern periphery of the Iranian world, now part of Afghanistan, Tajikistan, Uzbekistan, and, as a smaller part, Turkmenistan. The region was once host to religions like Zoroastrianism and Buddhism.
Achaemenid Empire	The Achaemenid Empire was the successor state of the Median Empire, expanding to eventually rule over significant portions of the ancient world which at around 500 B.C.E.

stretched from the Indus Valley in the east, to Thrace and Macedon on the northeastern border of Greece. The Achaemenid Empire would eventually control Egypt, encompassing some 1 million square miles unified by a complex network of roads, ruled by monarchs, to become the largest the world had yet seen.

Last Judgment

The Last Judgment is a canonical fresco by the Italian Renaissance master Michelangelo executed on the altar wall of the Sistine Chapel in Vatican City. The work took four years to complete and was done between 1536 and 1541 (preparation of the altar wall began in 1535). Michelangelo began working on it some twenty years after having finished the Sistine Chapel ceiling.

CHAPTER QUIZ: KEY TERMS, PEOPLE, PLACES, CONCEPTS

1. 35°23′53″E? / ?33.56056°N 35.39806°E? / 33.56056; 35.39806

_________,or Saïda, is the third-largest city in Lebanon. It is located in the South Governorate of Lebanon, on the Mediterranean coast, about 40 km (25 mi) north of Tyre and 40 km (25 mi) south of the capital Beirut. Its name means a fishery.

a. Erik the Red
b. Proto-Elamite
c. River civilization
d. Sidon

2. A _________ is a long prose narrative that describes fictional characters and events in the form of a sequential story, usually. The genre has historical roots in the fields of medieval and early modern romance and in the tradition of the novella. The latter, an Italian word used to describe short stories, supplied the present generic English term in the 18th century.

a. Second Servile War
b. Phoenicia
c. Postclassical Era
d. Novel

3. . Christian _________ is a religious observance celebrated by some churches to keep faith with Old Testament teaching. It is often linked to the Christian holiday and festival of Easter. Often, only an abbreviated seder is celebrated to explain the meaning in a time-limited ceremony.

a. Whitsun
b. Homily
c. Kerygma

4. 32°E? / ?39°N 32°E? / 39; 32

 _________ (from Greek ?νατολ? Anatole -- 'east' or '(sun)rise'; also Asia Minor, from Greek: Μικρ? ?σ?α Mikrá Asía 'small Asia'; in modern Turkish: Anadolu) is a geographic and historical term denoting the westernmost protrusion of Asia, comprising the majority of the Republic of Turkey. The region is bounded by the Black Sea to the north, Georgia to the northeast, the Armenian Highland to the east, Mesopotamia to the southeast, the Mediterranean Sea to the south and the Aegean Sea to the west. _________ has been home to many civilizations throughout history, such as the Hittites, Phrygians, Lydians, Persians, Greeks, Assyrians, Armenians, Romans, Byzantines, Anatolian Seljuks and Ottomans.

 a. Argishti II
 b. Armeno-Phrygian
 c. Anatolia
 d. Economic Stimulus Act of 2008

5. _________ or On Religious Power and Judaism (original: „_________ oder über religiöse Macht und Judentum') is the title of a book written by Moses Mendelssohn, which was first published in 1783 - the same year, when the Prussian officer Christian Wilhelm von Dohm published the second part of his Mémoire Concerning the amelioration of the civil status of the Jews. Moses Mendelssohn was one of the key figures of Jewish Enlightenment (Haskalah) and his philosophical treatise, dealing with social contract and political theory (especially concerning the question of the separation between religion and state), can be regarded as his most important contribution to Haskalah. The book which was written in Prussia on the eve of the French Revolution, consisted of two parts and each one was paged separately.

 a. Mutaween
 b. Jerusalem
 c. Political theology
 d. Public menorah

ANSWER KEY

2. Small Kingdoms and Mighty Empires in the Near East, ca. 1100-513B.C.E.

1. d

2. d

3. d

4. c

5. b

You can take the complete Chapter Practice Test

for 2. Small Kingdoms and Mighty Empires in the Near East, ca. 1100-513B.C.E.
on all key terms, persons, places, and concepts.

Online 99 Cents

http://www.epub141.56.21995.2.cram101.com/

Use www.Cram101.com for all your study needs

including Cram101's online interactive problem solving labs in

chemistry, statistics, mathematics, and more.

3. The Development of Classical Greece, ca. 2000-338B.C.E.

CHAPTER OUTLINE: KEY TERMS, PEOPLE, PLACES, CONCEPTS

- Classical period
- Athens
- Minoan civilization
- Mycenae
- Hesiod
- Iliad
- Odyssey
- Achilles
- Agamemnon
- Acropolis
- Agora
- Zeus
- Colonization
- First Messenian War
- Messenia
- Second Messenian War
- Sparta
- Draco
- Cimon
- Delian League
- Pausanias

3. The Development of Classical Greece, ca. 2000-338B.C.E.

CHAPTER OUTLINE: KEY TERMS, PEOPLE, PLACES, CONCEPTS

- Themistocles
- Peace of Nicias
- Peloponnesian War
- Pericles
- Potidaea
- Erechtheum
- Parthenon
- Aeschylus
- Euripides
- Sophocles
- Archilochus
- Aristotle
- Lesbian
- Sappho
- Aspasia
- Miletus
- Eleusinian Mysteries
- Hera
- Pythian Games
- Hegemony
- Epaminondas

CHAPTER OUTLINE: KEY TERMS, PEOPLE, PLACES, CONCEPTS

______________	Macedonia

CHAPTER HIGHLIGHTS & NOTES: KEY TERMS, PEOPLE, PLACES, CONCEPTS

Classical period

The dates of the Classical Period in Western music are generally accepted as being between about 1750 and 1830. However, the term classical music is used colloquially to describe a variety of Western musical styles from the ninth century to the present, and especially from the sixteenth or seventeenth to the nineteenth

The Classical period falls between the Baroque and the Romantic periods.

Athens

Athens is the capital and largest city of Greece. Athens dominates the Attica periphery and it is one of the world's oldest cities, as its recorded history spans around 3,400 years.

The Greek capital has a population of 745,514 (in 2001) within its administrative limits and a land area of 39 km^2 (15 sq mi).

Minoan civilization

The Minoan civilization was a Bronze Age civilization that arose on the island of Crete and flourished from approximately the 27th century BCE to the 15th century BCE. It was rediscovered at the beginning of the 20th century through the work of the British archaeologist Arthur Evans. Will Durant referred to it as 'the first link in the European chain.'

The early inhabitants of Crete settled as early as 128,000 BCE, during the Middle Paleolithic age. It was not until 5000 BCE that the first signs of advanced agriculture appeared, marking the beginning of civilization.

Mycenae

Mycenae is an archaeological site in Greece, located about 90 km southwest of Athens, in the north-eastern Peloponnese. Argos is 11 km to the south; Corinth, 48 km to the north. From the hill on which the palace was located one can see across the Argolid to the Saronic Gulf.

Hesiod

Hesiod was a Greek oral poet generally thought by scholars to have been active between 750 and 650 BC, around the same time as Homer. His is the first European poetry in which the poet regards himself as a topic, an individual with a distinctive role to play. Ancient authors credited him and Homer with establishing Greek religious customs.

Iliad

The Iliad is an epic poem in dactylic hexameters, traditionally attributed to Homer.

Set during the Trojan War, the ten-year siege of the city of Troy (Ilium) by a coalition of Greek states, it tells of the battles and events during the weeks of a quarrel between King Agamemnon and the warrior Achilles. Although the story covers only a few weeks in the final year of the war, the Iliad mentions or alludes to many of the Greek legends about the siege, the earlier events, such as the gathering of warriors for the siege, the cause of the war and similar, tending to appear near the beginning, and the events prophesied for the future, such as Achilles' looming death and the sack of Troy, prefigured and alluded to more and more vividly approaching the end of the poem, making the poem tell a more or less complete tale of the Trojan War.

Odyssey

The Odyssey is one of two major ancient Greek epic poems attributed to Homer. It is, in part, a sequel to the Iliad, the other work traditionally ascribed to Homer. The poem is fundamental to the modern Western canon.

Achilles

In Greek mythology, Achilles was a Greek hero of the Trojan War, the central character and the greatest warrior of Homer's Iliad.

Achilles also has the attributes of being the most handsome of the heroes assembled against Troy.

Later legends (beginning with a poem by Statius in the 1st century AD) state that Achilles was invulnerable in all of his body except for his heel.

Agamemnon

In Greek mythology, Agamemnon was the son of King Atreus of Mycenae and Queen Aerope; the brother of Menelaus and the husband of Clytemnestra; mythical legends make him the king of Mycenae or Argos, thought to be different names for the same area. When Helen, the wife of Menelaus, was abducted by Paris of Troy, Agamemnon was the commander of the Achaeans in the ensuing Trojan War.

Upon Agamemnon's return from Troy he was murdered (according to the fullest version of the oldest surviving account, Odyssey Book 11, l.409f).

Acropolis

An acropolis is a settlement, especially a citadel, built upon an area of elevated ground-frequently a hill with precipitous sides, chosen for purposes of defense. In many parts of the world, acropoleis became the nuclei of large cities of classical antiquity, such as ancient Rome, which in more recent times grew up on the surrounding lower ground, such as modern Rome.

The word acropolis literally in Greek means 'city on the extremity' and though associated primarily with the Greek cities Athens, Argos, Thebes, and Corinth (with its Acrocorinth), may be applied generically to all such citadels, including Rome, Jerusalem, Celtic Bratislava, many in Asia Minor, or even Castle Rock in Edinburgh.

Agora

Agora is a 2009 Spanish English-language historical drama film directed by Alejandro Amenábar and written by Amenábar and Mateo Gil.

The biopic stars Rachel Weisz as Hypatia, a female mathematician, philosopher and astronomer in late 4th century Roman Egypt, who investigates the flaws of the geocentric Ptolemaic system and the heliocentric model that challenges it. Surrounded by religious turmoil and social unrest, Hypatia struggles to save the knowledge of classical antiquity from destruction.

Zeus

In Greek mythology Zeus is the 'Father of Gods and men', according to Hesiod's Theogony, who ruled the Olympians of Mount Olympus as a father ruled the family; he was the god of sky and thunder in Greek mythology. As Walter Burkert points out in his book, Greek Religion, 'Even the gods who are not his natural children address him as Father, and all the gods rise in his presence.' (Iliad, book 1.503;533). For the Greeks, he was the King of the Gods, who oversaw the universe.

Colonization

Colonization occurs whenever any one or more species populate an area. The term, which is derived from the Latin colere, 'to inhabit, cultivate, frequent practice, tend, guard, respect', originally referred to humans. During the 19th century, biogeographers appropriated the term to also describe the activities of birds, bacteria, or plant species.

First Messenian War

The First Messenian War was a war between Messenia and Sparta. It began in 743 BC and ended in 724 BC, according to the dates given by Pausanias.

The war continued the rivalry between the Achaeans and the Dorians that had been initiated by the Return of the Heracleidae (Dorian Invasion).

Messenia

Messenia or Messinia was an ancient district the south-western part of the Peloponnese. To the north it had a border with Elis along the Neda river, from whence the border with Arcadia ran along the tops of Mount Elaeum and Mount Nomia. The northern border with Arcadia then ran amongst the foothills of Taygetos, but all the headwater of the Alpheios river lay outside Messenia.

Second Messenian War

The Second Messenian War was a war between the Ancient Greek states of Messenia and Sparta. It started around 40 years after the end of the First Messenian War with the uprising of a slave rebellion. This war lasted from 685 to 668 BC. Prelude

The First Messenian War lasted from 743 BC to 724 BC. Sparta at the time prior to conquest dealt with overpopulation in the Laconia region.

Sparta

ΣPARTA is a semiannual educational magazine dedicated to the ancient Spartan and Greek history, with a readership that mainly represent teachers, historians, re-enactors and other individuals interested in the history of ancient Greece.

The magazine is published by Markoulakis Publications.

It is mainly distributed in the United Kingdom, but was also marketed in Europe, Canada, and the USA. The magazine initially appeared as an open access journal entitled Sparta's Journal (ISSN 1747-0005]) in 2004. The first print issue of ΣPARTA had June 2006 as cover-date.

Draco

Draco was the first legislator of ancient Athens, Greece, 7th century BC. He replaced the prevailing system of oral law and blood feud by a written code to be enforced only by a court. Because of its harshness, this code also gave rise to the term 'draconian'.

During the 39th Olympiad, in 622 or 621 BC, Draco established the legal code with which he is identified.

Cimon

Cimon (510, Athens - 450 BC, Citium, Cyprus), was an Athenian statesman, strategos, and major political figure in mid-5th century BC Greece, the son of Miltiades, victor of Marathon. Cimon played a key role in creating the powerful Athenian maritime empire following the failure of the Persian invasion of Greece by Xerxes I in 480-479 BC. Cimon became a celebrated military hero and was elevated to the rank of admiral after fighting in the Battle of Salamis.

One of Cimon's greatest exploits was his destruction of a Persian fleet and army at the Battle of the Eurymedon river in 466 BC. In 462 BC, he led an unsuccessful expedition to support the Spartans during the helot uprisings.

Delian League

The Delian League, founded in 477 BC, was an association of Greek city-states, members numbering between 150 to 173, under the leadership of Athens, whose purpose was to continue fighting the Persian Empire after the Greek victory in the Battle of Plataea at the end of the Greco-Persian Wars. Shortly after its inception, Athens began to exploit the League's navy for its own benefit. This behavior would frequently lead to conflict between Athens and the less powerful members of the League.

Pausanias

Pausanias (died c. 470 BC) was a Spartan general of the 5th century BC. He was a scion of the royal house of the Agiads but not in the direct line of succession himself: the son of Cleombrotus and nephew of Leonidas I, serving as regent after the latter's death, since Leonidas' son Pleistarchus was still under-age. Pausanias was also the father of Pleistoanax, who later became king, and Cleomenes. Pausanias was responsible for the Greek victory over Mardonius and the Persians at the Battle of Plataea in 479 BC, and was the leader of the Hellenic League created to resist Persian aggression during the Greco-Persian Wars.

Themistocles

Themistocles was an Athenian politician and general. He was one of a new breed of non-aristocratic politicians who rose to prominence in the early years of the Athenian democracy. As a politician, Themistocles was a populist, having the support of lower class Athenians, and generally being at odds with the Athenian nobility.

Visit Cram101.com for full Practice Exams

Peace of Nicias

The Peace of Nicias was a peace treaty signed between the Greek city-states of Athens and Sparta in the March of 421 BC, ending the first half of the Peloponnesian War.

In 425 BC, the Spartans had lost the battles of Pylos and Sphacteria, a severe defeat resulting in the Athenians holding 292 prisoners. At least 120 were Spartiates.

Peloponnesian War

The Peloponnesian War, 431 to 404 BC, was an ancient Greek war fought by Athens and its empire against the Peloponnesian League led by Sparta. Historians have traditionally divided the war into three phases. In the first phase, the Archidamian War, Sparta launched repeated invasions of Attica, while Athens took advantage of its naval supremacy to raid the coast of the Peloponnese attempting to suppress signs of unrest in its empire. This period of the war was concluded in 421 BC, with the signing of the Peace of Nicias. That treaty, however, was soon undermined by renewed fighting in the Peloponnese. In 415 BC, Athens dispatched a massive expeditionary force to attack Syracuse in Sicily; the attack failed disastrously, with the destruction of the entire force, in 413 BC. This ushered in the final phase of the war, generally referred to either as the Decelean War, or the Ionian War. In this phase, Sparta, now receiving support from Persia, supported rebellions in Athens' subject states in the Aegean Sea and Ionia, undermining Athens' empire, and, eventually, depriving the city of naval supremacy. The destruction of Athens' fleet at Aegospotami effectively ended the war, and Athens surrendered in the following year.

Pericles

Pericles was the most prominent and influential Greek statesmen, orator, and general of Athens during the Golden Age-specifically, the time between the Persian and Peloponnesian wars. He was descended, through his mother, from the powerful and historically influential Alcmaeonid family.

Pericles had such a profound influence on Athenian society that Thucydides, his contemporary historian, acclaimed him as 'the first citizen of Athens'.

Potidaea

Potidaea was a colony founded by the Corinthians around 600 BC in the narrowest point of the peninsula of Pallene, the westernmost of three peninsulas at the southern end of Chalcidice in northern Greece.

While besieged by the Persians in 479 BC, the town was saved by the earliest recorded tsunami in history. Herodotus reports how the Persians attackers who tried to exploit an unusual retreat of the water were suddenly surprised by 'a great flood-tide, higher, as the people of the place say, than any one of the many that had been before'.

Erechtheum

The Erechtheum or Erechtheion is an ancient Greek temple on the north side of the Acropolis of Athens in Greece.

Architecture

The temple as seen today was built between 421 and 406 BC.

Its architect may have been Mnesicles, and it derived its name from a shrine dedicated to the legendary Greek hero Erichthonius. The sculptor and mason of the structure was Phidias, who was employed by Pericles to build both the Erechtheum and the Parthenon.

Parthenon

The Parthenon is a temple on the Athenian Acropolis, Greece, dedicated to the Greek goddess Athena, whom the people of Athens considered their patron. Its construction began in 447 BC and was completed in 438 BC, although decorations of the Parthenon continued until 432 BC. It is the most important surviving building of Classical Greece, generally considered to be the culmination of the development of the Doric order. Its decorative sculptures are considered some of the high points of Greek art.

Aeschylus

Aeschylus was the first of the three ancient Greek tragedians whose plays can still be read or performed, the others being Sophocles and Euripides. He is often described as the father of tragedy: our knowledge of the genre begins with his work and our understanding of earlier tragedies is largely based on inferences from his surviving plays. According to Aristotle, he expanded the number of characters in plays to allow for conflict amongst them, whereas previously characters had interacted only with the chorus.

Euripides

Euripides (c. 480 - 406 BC) was one of the three great tragedians of classical Athens, the other two being Aeschylus and Sophocles. Some ancient scholars attributed ninety-five plays to him but according to the Suda it was ninety-two at most. Of these, eighteen or nineteen have survived complete (there has been debate about his authorship of Rhesus, largely on stylistic grounds) and there are also fragments, some substantial, of most of the other plays.

Sophocles

Sophocles is one of three ancient Greek tragedians whose plays have survived. His first plays were written later than those of Aeschylus, and earlier than or contemporary with those of Euripides. According to the Suda, a 10th century encyclopedia, Sophocles wrote 123 plays during the course of his life, but only seven have survived in a complete form: Ajax, Antigone, The Women of Trachis, Oedipus the King, Electra, Philoctetes and Oedipus at Colonus.

Archilochus

Archilochus, Archilochos (c. 680 BC - c. 645 BC) was a poet from the island of Paros in the Archaic period in Greece celebrated for his versatile and innovative use of poetic meters and as the earliest known Greek author to compose almost entirely on the theme of his own emotions and experiences. Alexandrian scholars included him in their canonic list of iambic poets, along with Semonides and Hipponax, yet ancient commentators also numbered him with Tyrtaeus and Callinus as the possible inventor of the elegy. However modern critics often characterize him simply as a lyric poet.

Aristotle

Aristotle (384 BC - 322 BC) was a Greek philosopher and polymath, a student of Plato and teacher of Alexander the Great.

His writings cover many subjects, including physics, metaphysics, poetry, theater, music, logic, rhetoric, linguistics, politics, government, ethics, biology, and zoology. Together with Plato and Socrates (Plato's teacher), Aristotle is one of the most important founding figures in Western philosophy.

Lesbian

Lesbian is a term most widely used in the English language to describe sexual and romantic desire between females. The word may be used as a noun, to refer to women who identify themselves or who are characterized by others as having the primary attribute of female homosexuality, or as an adjective, to describe characteristics of an object or activity related to female same-sex desire.

Lesbian as a concept, used to differentiate women with a shared sexual orientation, is a 20th-century construct.

Sappho

Sappho was an Ancient Greek poet, born on the island of Lesbos. Later Greeks included her in the list of nine lyric poets. Her birth was sometime between 630 and 612 BC, and it is said that she died around 570 BC, but little is known for certain about her life. The bulk of her poetry, which was well-known and greatly admired throughout antiquity, has been lost, but her immense reputation has endured through surviving fragments.

Aspasia

Aspasia was a Milesian woman who was famous for her involvement with the Athenian statesman Pericles. Very little is known about the details of her life. She spent most of her adult life in Athens, and she may have influenced Pericles and Athenian politics.

Miletus

Miletus was a character from Greek mythology.

Miletus was son of Apollo and Areia, daughter of Cleochus, of Crete. Another tradition relates that Miletus was the son of Akakallis, the daughter of Minos, with Apollo.

Eleusinian Mysteries

The Eleusinian Mysteries were initiation ceremonies held every year for the cult of Demeter and Persephone based at Eleusis in ancient Greece. Of all the mysteries celebrated in ancient times, these were held to be the ones of greatest importance. It is acknowledged that their basis was an old agrarian cult which probably goes back to the Mycenean period (c.1600-1100 BC) and it is believed that the cult of Demeter was established in 1500 BC. The idea of immortality which appears in syncretistic religions of antiquity was introduced in late antiquity.

Hera

Hera was the wife and one of three sisters of Zeus in the Olympian pantheon of classical Greek Mythology. Her chief function was as the goddess of women and marriage. In Roman mythology, Juno was the equivalent mythical character.

Pythian Games

The Pythian Games were one of the four Panhellenic Games of Ancient Greece, a forerunner of the modern Olympic Games, held every four years at the sanctuary of Apollo at Delphi.

They were held in honour of Apollo two years after (and two years before) each Olympic Games, and between each Nemean and Isthmian Games. They were founded sometime in the 6th century BCE, and, unlike the Olympic Games, also featured competitions for art and dance.

Hegemony

Hegemony is an indirect form of imperial dominance in which the hegemon (leader state) rules sub-ordinate states by the implied means of power rather than direct military force. In Ancient Greece (8th c. BC - AD 6th c)., hegemony denoted the politico-military dominance of a city-state over other city-states.

Epaminondas

Epaminondas was a Theban general and statesman of the 4th century BC who transformed the Ancient Greek city-state of Thebes, leading it out of Spartan subjugation into a preeminent position in Greek politics. In the process he broke Spartan military power with his victory at Leuctra and liberated the Messenian helots, a group of Peloponnesian Greeks who had been enslaved under Spartan rule for some 230 years, having been defeated in the Messenian War ending in 600 BC. Epaminondas reshaped the political map of Greece, fragmented old alliances, created new ones, and supervised the construction of entire cities. He was militarily influential as well, inventing and implementing several major battlefield tactics.

Macedonia

Macedonia was an ancient Greek kingdom. The kingdom, centered in the northeastern part of the Greek peninsula, was bordered by Epirus to the west, Paeonia to the north, the region of Thrace to the east and Thessaly to the south. The rise of Macedon, from a small kingdom at the periphery of Classical Greek affairs, to one which came to dominate the entire Hellenic world, occurred under the reign of Philip II. For a brief period, after the conquests of Alexander the Great, it became the most powerful state in the world, controlling a territory that included the former Persian Empire, stretching as far as the Indus River; at that time it inaugurated the Hellenistic period of Ancient Greek civilization.

Visit Cram101.com for full Practice Exams

1. _________ was the first of the three ancient Greek tragedians whose plays can still be read or performed, the others being Sophocles and Euripides. He is often described as the father of tragedy: our knowledge of the genre begins with his work and our understanding of earlier tragedies is largely based on inferences from his surviving plays. According to Aristotle, he expanded the number of characters in plays to allow for conflict amongst them, whereas previously characters had interacted only with the chorus.

   a. Artapanus
   b. Artaphernes
   c. Artayctes
   d. Aeschylus

2. _________ is a 2009 Spanish English-language historical drama film directed by Alejandro Amenábar and written by Amenábar and Mateo Gil. The biopic stars Rachel Weisz as Hypatia, a female mathematician, philosopher and astronomer in late 4th century Roman Egypt, who investigates the flaws of the geocentric Ptolemaic system and the heliocentric model that challenges it. Surrounded by religious turmoil and social unrest, Hypatia struggles to save the knowledge of classical antiquity from destruction.

   a. Agora
   b. Emeth
   c. Unclean spirit
   d. Pagae

3. _________ was a Greek oral poet generally thought by scholars to have been active between 750 and 650 BC, around the same time as Homer. His is the first European poetry in which the poet regards himself as a topic, an individual with a distinctive role to play. Ancient authors credited him and Homer with establishing Greek religious customs.

   a. Erik the Red
   b. Hesiod
   c. Nichoria
   d. Pagae

4. _________ is the capital and largest city of Greece. _________ dominates the Attica periphery and it is one of the world's oldest cities, as its recorded history spans around 3,400 years.

   The Greek capital has a population of 745,514 (in 2001) within its administrative limits and a land area of 39 km^2 (15 sq mi).

   a. Athens
   b. Sheraton style
   c. Baptism of Poland
   d. History of Christianity in Ukraine

5. . _________ is one of three ancient Greek tragedians whose plays have survived. His first plays were written later than those of Aeschylus, and earlier than or contemporary with those of Euripides.

According to the Suda, a 10th century encyclopedia, _________ wrote 123 plays during the course of his life, but only seven have survived in a complete form: Ajax, Antigone, The Women of Trachis, Oedipus the King, Electra, Philoctetes and Oedipus at Colonus.

a. Xenocles
b. Sophocles
c. Julia Antonia
d. Pratinas

Visit Cram101.com for full Practice Exams

ANSWER KEY
3. The Development of Classical Greece, ca. 2000-338B.C.E.

1. d
2. a
3. b
4. a
5. b

You can take the complete Chapter Practice Test

for 3. The Development of Classical Greece, ca. 2000-338B.C.E.
on all key terms, persons, places, and concepts.

Online 99 Cents

http://www.epub141.56.21995.3.cram101.com/

Use www.Cram101.com for all your study needs

including Cram101's online interactive problem solving labs in

chemistry, statistics, mathematics, and more.

4. The Hellenistic World, 336-30B.C.E.

CHAPTER OUTLINE: KEY TERMS, PEOPLE, PLACES, CONCEPTS

Battle of Issus

Achaemenid Empire

Agora

Antigonid dynasty

Achaean League

Aetolian League

Bactria

Ptolemy

Plutarch

Altar

Hellenization

Silk Road

Zeus

Cult

Stoicism

Eratosthenes

Palimpsest

Erasistratus

Heraclides of Tarentum

Visit Cram101.com for full Practice Exams

4. The Hellenistic World, 336-30B.C.E.

Battle of Issus

The Battle of Issus occurred in southern Anatolia, in November 333 BC. The invading Macedonian troops, led by Alexander the Great, defeated an army led by Darius III of Achaemenid Persia in the second great battle of Alexander's conquest of Asia. After the Macedonians soundly defeated the Persian satraps of Asia Minor at the Battle of the Granicus, Darius took personal command of his army. He gathered reinforcements and led his men in a surprise march behind the Macedonian advance to cut their line of supply.

Achaemenid Empire

The Achaemenid Empire was the successor state of the Median Empire, expanding to eventually rule over significant portions of the ancient world which at around 500 B.C.E. stretched from the Indus Valley in the east, to Thrace and Macedon on the northeastern border of Greece. The Achaemenid Empire would eventually control Egypt, encompassing some 1 million square miles unified by a complex network of roads, ruled by monarchs, to become the largest the world had yet seen.

Agora

Agora is a 2009 Spanish English-language historical drama film directed by Alejandro Amenábar and written by Amenábar and Mateo Gil. The biopic stars Rachel Weisz as Hypatia, a female mathematician, philosopher and astronomer in late 4th century Roman Egypt, who investigates the flaws of the geocentric Ptolemaic system and the heliocentric model that challenges it. Surrounded by religious turmoil and social unrest, Hypatia struggles to save the knowledge of classical antiquity from destruction.

Antigonid dynasty

The Antigonid dynasty was a dynasty of Hellenistic kings descended from Alexander the Great's general Antigonus I Monophthalmus ('the One-eyed').

History

Succeeding the Antipatrid dynasty in much of Macedonia, Antigonus ruled mostly over Asia Minor and northern Syria. His attempts to take control of the whole of Alexander's empire led to his defeat and death at the Battle of Ipsus in 301 BC. Antigonus's son Demetrius I Poliorcetes survived the battle, and managed to seize control of Macedon itself a few years later, but eventually lost his throne, dying in prison.

Achaean League

The Achaean League was a Hellenistic era confederation of Greek city states on the northern and central Peloponnese, which existed between 280 BC and 146 BC.

The regional Achaean League was reformed in 281/0 BC (on the basis of a looser alliance of the founding city-states extending back to the 5th century BC), and soon expanded beyond its Achaean heartland. It was first joined by the city of Sicyon in 251, which provided it with its first great leader, Aratus of Sicyon.

Visit Cram101.com for full Practice Exams

Aetolian League	The Aetolian League was a confederation of tribal communities and cities in ancient Greece centered on Aetolia in central Greece. It was established, probably during the early Hellenistic era, in opposition to Macedon and the Achaean League. Two annual meetings were held in Thermika and Panaetolika.
Bactria	Bactria, later variously Tukharistan, Tokharistan, and Tocharistan, was the ancient name of a historical region in Central Asia, located between the range of the Hindu Kush and the Amu Darya (Oxus). It was a part of the northeastern periphery of the Iranian world, now part of Afghanistan, Tajikistan, Uzbekistan, and, as a smaller part, Turkmenistan. The region was once host to religions like Zoroastrianism and Buddhism.
Ptolemy	The name Ptolemy or Ptolemaeus comes from the Greek Ptolemaios, which means warlike. There have been many people named Ptolemy or Ptolemaeus, the most famous of which are the Greek-Egyptian astronomer Claudius Ptolemaeus and the Macedonian founder and ruler of the Ptolemaic Kingdom in Egypt, Ptolemy I Soter. The following sections summarise the history of the name, some of the people named Ptolemy, and some of the other uses of this name.
Plutarch	Plutarch, born Plutarchos then named, on his becoming a Roman citizen, Lucius Mestrius Plutarchus , c. 46 - 120 CE, was a Greek historian, biographer, essayist, and Middle Platonist known primarily for his Parallel Lives and Moralia. He was born to a prominent family in Chaeronea, Boeotia, a town about twenty miles east of Delphi. Early life Plutarch was born in 46 CE in the small town of Chaeronea, in the Greek region known as Boeotia.
Altar	In the liturgy of the Roman Rite of the Catholic Church, the altar is where the Sacrifice of the Mass is offered. Mass may sometimes be celebrated outside a sacred place, but never without an altar, or at least an altar stone. In ecclesiastical history we find only two exceptions: St. Lucian (312) is said to have celebrated Mass on his breast whilst in prison, and Theodore, Bishop of Tyre on the hands of his deacons.
Hellenization	Hellenization is a term used to describe the spread of ancient Greek culture, and, to a lesser extent, language, over foreign peoples conquered by Greece or in its sphere of influence. It is mainly used to describe the spread of Hellenistic civilization during the Hellenistic period following the campaigns of Alexander the Great of Macedon. The result of Hellenization was that elements of Greek origin combined in various forms and degrees with local elements, which is known as Hellenism.

4. The Hellenistic World, 336-30B.C.E.

Silk Road

The Silk Road or Silk Route is a modern term referring to a historical network of interlinking trade routes across the Afro-Eurasian landmass that connected East, South, and Western Asia with the Mediterranean and European world, as well as parts of North and East Africa. Extending 4,000 miles (6,500 km), the Silk Road gets its name from the lucrative Chinese silk trade along it, which began during the Han Dynasty (206 BC - 220 AD). The central Asian sections of the trade routes were expanded around 114 BC by the Han dynasty, largely through the missions and explorations of Zhang Qian, but earlier trade routes across the continents already existed.

Trade on the Silk Road was a significant factor in the development of the civilizations of China, India, Persia, Europe and Arabia.

Zeus

In Greek mythology Zeus is the 'Father of Gods and men', according to Hesiod's Theogony, who ruled the Olympians of Mount Olympus as a father ruled the family; he was the god of sky and thunder in Greek mythology. As Walter Burkert points out in his book, Greek Religion, 'Even the gods who are not his natural children address him as Father, and all the gods rise in his presence.' (Iliad, book 1.503;533). For the Greeks, he was the King of the Gods, who oversaw the universe.

Cult

In traditional usage, the cult of a religion, quite apart from its sacred writings ('scriptures'), its theology or myths, or the personal faith of its believers, is the totality of external religious practice and observance, the neglect of which is the definition of impiety. Cult in this primary sense is literally the 'care' owed to the god and the shrine. In the specific context of Greek hero cult, Carla Antonaccio has written, 'The term cult identifies a pattern of ritual behavior in connection with specific objects, within a framework of spatial and temporal coordinates.

Stoicism

Stoicism is a school of Hellenistic philosophy founded in Athens by Zeno of Citium in the early 3rd century BC. The Stoics taught that destructive emotions resulted from errors in judgment, and that a sage, or person of 'moral and intellectual perfection,' would not suffer such emotions.

Stoics were concerned with the active relationship between cosmic determinism and human freedom, and the belief that it is virtuous to maintain a will (called prohairesis) that is in accord with nature. Because of this, the Stoics presented their philosophy as a way of life, and they thought that the best indication of an individual's philosophy was not what a person said but how he behaved.

Eratosthenes

Eratosthenes of Athens was one of the Thirty Tyrants elected to rule the city of Athens after the Peloponnesian War (431-404 BC).

Having lost the war to the Spartans, the citizens of Athens elected thirty men as oligarchs. These Thirty instituted oppressive and highly exclusionary laws and instituted a political purge against Athenians who had been Spartan informers and collaborators during the long war.

CHAPTER HIGHLIGHTS & NOTES: KEY TERMS, PEOPLE, PLACES, CONCEPTS

Palimpsest

A palimpsest is a manuscript page from a scroll or book from which the text has been scraped or washed off and which can be used again. The word 'palimpsest' comes through Latin palimpsestus from Ancient Greek παλ?μψηστος (palímpsestos, 'scratched or scraped again') originally compounded from π?λιν (palin, 'again') and ψ?ω (psao, 'I scrape') literally meaning 'scraped clean and used again'. Romans wrote on wax-coated tablets that could be smoothed and reused, and a passing use of the term 'palimpsest' by Cicero seems to refer to this practice.

Erasistratus

Erasistratus was a Greek anatomist and royal physician under Seleucus I Nicator of Syria. Along with fellow physician Herophilus, he founded a school of anatomy in Alexandria, where they carried out anatomical research. He is credited for his description of the valves of the heart, and he also concluded that the heart was not the center of sensations, but instead it functioned as a pump.

Heraclides of Tarentum

Heraclides of Tarentum, (c. 2nd century BC), was a Greek physician of the Empiric school who wrote commentaries on the works of Hippocrates.

He came from Tarentum, was a pupil of Mantias, and probably lived in the 3rd or 2nd century BC, somewhat later than Apollonius Empiricus and Glaucias. He belonged to the Empiric school, and wrote some works on Materia medica, which are very frequently quoted by Galen, but of which only a few fragments remain.

CHAPTER QUIZ: KEY TERMS, PEOPLE, PLACES, CONCEPTS

1. In Greek mythology _________ is the 'Father of Gods and men', according to Hesiod's Theogony, who ruled the Olympians of Mount Olympus as a father ruled the family; he was the god of sky and thunder in Greek mythology. As Walter Burkert points out in his book, Greek Religion, 'Even the gods who are not his natural children address him as Father, and all the gods rise in his presence.' (Iliad, book 1.503;533). For the Greeks, he was the King of the Gods, who oversaw the universe.

   a. Jupiter Tonans
   b. Second Servile War
   c. History of Christianity in Ukraine
   d. Zeus

2. . _________, born Plutarchos then named, on his becoming a Roman citizen, Lucius Mestrius Plutarchus , c. 46 - 120 CE, was a Greek historian, biographer, essayist, and Middle Platonist known primarily for his Parallel Lives and Moralia. He was born to a prominent family in Chaeronea, Boeotia, a town about twenty miles east of Delphi.

   Early life

_________ was born in 46 CE in the small town of Chaeronea, in the Greek region known as Boeotia.

a. Arrian
b. Plutarch
c. Julia Antonia
d. Travelling menagerie

3. _________ is a term used to describe the spread of ancient Greek culture, and, to a lesser extent, language, over foreign peoples conquered by Greece or in its sphere of influence. It is mainly used to describe the spread of Hellenistic civilization during the Hellenistic period following the campaigns of Alexander the Great of Macedon. The result of _________ was that elements of Greek origin combined in various forms and degrees with local elements, which is known as Hellenism.

a. Hellenization
b. Minorities in Greece
c. Muslim minority of Greece
d. Scuola dei Greci

4. The _________ or Silk Route is a modern term referring to a historical network of interlinking trade routes across the Afro-Eurasian landmass that connected East, South, and Western Asia with the Mediterranean and European world, as well as parts of North and East Africa. Extending 4,000 miles (6,500 km), the _________ gets its name from the lucrative Chinese silk trade along it, which began during the Han Dynasty (206 BC - 220 AD). The central Asian sections of the trade routes were expanded around 114 BC by the Han dynasty, largely through the missions and explorations of Zhang Qian, but earlier trade routes across the continents already existed.

Trade on the _________ was a significant factor in the development of the civilizations of China, India, Persia, Europe and Arabia.

a. Dharmaguptaka
b. Silk
c. Erik the Red
d. Silk Road

5. . _________ is a 2009 Spanish English-language historical drama film directed by Alejandro Amenábar and written by Amenábar and Mateo Gil. The biopic stars Rachel Weisz as Hypatia, a female mathematician, philosopher and astronomer in late 4th century Roman Egypt, who investigates the flaws of the geocentric Ptolemaic system and the heliocentric model that challenges it. Surrounded by religious turmoil and social unrest, Hypatia struggles to save the knowledge of classical antiquity from destruction.

a. Agora
b. Emeth
c. Unclean spirit

Visit Cram101.com for full Practice Exams

ANSWER KEY
4. The Hellenistic World, 336-30B.C.E.

1. d
2. b
3. a
4. d
5. a

You can take the complete Chapter Practice Test

for 4. The Hellenistic World, 336-30B.C.E.
on all key terms, persons, places, and concepts.

Online 99 Cents

http://www.epub141.56.21995.4.cram101.com/

Use www.Cram101.com for all your study needs

including Cram101's online interactive problem solving labs in

chemistry, statistics, mathematics, and more.

5. The Rise of Rome, ca. 750-31B.C.E.

CHAPTER OUTLINE: KEY TERMS, PEOPLE, PLACES, CONCEPTS

Roman Republic

Aedile

Patrician

Praetor

Lex Canuleia

Gauls

Carthage

Epirus

First Punic War

Punic Wars

Achaean League

Sallust

Cato the Elder

Pax Romana

Scipio Aemilianus

Third Punic War

Hera

Zeus

Pontifex Maximus

Jugurtha

Numidia

Visit Cram101.com for full Practice Exams

5. The Rise of Rome, ca. 750-31B.C.E.

CHAPTER OUTLINE: KEY TERMS, PEOPLE, PLACES, CONCEPTS

______	Teutons
______	Julius Caesar
______	Social War
______	Cisalpine Gaul
______	Ides of March
______	Second Triumvirate

CHAPTER HIGHLIGHTS & NOTES: KEY TERMS, PEOPLE, PLACES, CONCEPTS

Roman Republic	The Roman Republic was a state declared on February 9, 1849, when the government of Papal States was temporarily replaced by a republican government due to Pope Pius IX's flight to Gaeta. The republic was led by Carlo Armellini, Giuseppe Mazzini and Aurelio Saffi. Together they formed a triumvirate, a reflection of a form of government seen in the ancient Roman Republic.
Aedile	Aedile was an office of the Roman Republic. Based in Rome, the aediles were responsible for maintenance of public buildings and regulation of public festivals. They also had powers to enforce public order.
Patrician	Patricianship, the quality of belonging to a patriciate, began in the ancient world, where cities such as Ancient Rome had a class of patrician families whose members were the only people allowed to exercise many political functions. In the rise of European towns in the tenth and eleventh centuries, the patriciate, a limited group of families with a special constitutional position, in Henri Pirenne's view, was the motive force. In 19th century central Europe, the term had become synonymous with the Bourgeoisie.
Praetor	Praetor was a title granted by the government of Ancient Rome to men acting in one of two official capacities: The commander of an army, usually in the field, or the named commander before mustering the army; and an elected magistratus (magistrate) assigned varied duties (per the historical period). The functions of the magistracy, the praetura (praetorship), are described by the adjective: the praetoria potestas (praetorian power), the praetorium imperium (praetorian authority), and the praetorium ius (praetorian law), the legal precedents established by the praetori (praetors).

Lex Canuleia

The Lex Canuleia is a law of the Roman Republic passed in the year 445 BC. Named after the tribune Gaius Canuleius, who proposed it, it abolished a corresponding prohibition in the Twelve Tables and allowed marriage between patricians and plebeians, with children inheriting the father's social status. It is also referred to in Latin as the Lex de conubio patrum et plebis.

Canuleius also carried through a law that permitted plebeians to hold the office of consul, the highest of the Roman magistracies, which the patricians had retained as their prerogative.

Gauls

The Gauls were a Celtic people living in Gaul, the region roughly corresponding to what is now France, Belgium, Switzerland and Northern Italy, from the Iron Age through the Roman period. They mostly spoke the Continental Celtic language called Gaulish.

Gauls under Brennus defeated Roman forces in a battle circa 390 BCE. The peak of Gaulish expansion was reached in the 3rd century BCE, in the wake of the Gallic invasion of the Balkans of 281-279 BCE, when Gaulish settlers moved as far afield as Asia Minor.

Carthage

Carthage is a suburb of Tunis, Tunisia, with a population of 20,715 (2004 census), and was the centre of the Carthaginian Empire in antiquity. The city has existed for nearly 3,000 years, developing from a Phoenician colony of the 1st millennium BC into the capital of an ancient empire.

Other spellings are: Latin: or, Ancient Greek: Karkhedon, Arabic: ? Qar?aj, Berber: Kartajen, Etruscan: *Carθaza, Modern Hebrew: ? Qartágo, from the Phoenician meaning New City , implying it was a 'new Tyre'.

Epirus

Epirus was an ancient Greek state, located in the geographical region of Epirus, in the western Balkans. The homeland of the ancient Epirotes was bordered by the Aetolian League to the south, Thessalia and Macedonia to the east, and Illyrian tribes to the north. For a brief period (280-275 BC), the Epirote leader Pyrrhus managed to make Epirus the most powerful state in the Greek world, and his armies marched against Rome during an unsuccessful campaign in Italy.

First Punic War

The First Punic War was the first of three wars fought between Ancient Carthage and the Roman Republic. For 20 years, the two powers struggled for supremacy in the western Mediterranean Sea, primarily on the Mediterranean island of Sicily and its surrounding waters but also to a lesser extent in the Apennine peninsula and North Africa. Carthage, located in what is today Tunisia, was the dominant Western Mediterranean power at the beginning of the conflicts. However, the Roman Republic eventually emerged as the victor, imposing strict treaty conditions and heavy financial penalties against Carthage.

Punic Wars

The Punic Wars were a series of three wars fought between Rome and Carthage from 264 B.C to 146 B.C. At the time, they were probably the largest wars that had ever taken place.

Visit Cram101.com for full Practice Exams

5. The Rise of Rome, ca. 750-31B.C.E.

CHAPTER HIGHLIGHTS & NOTES: KEY TERMS, PEOPLE, PLACES, CONCEPTS

Achaean League	The Achaean League was a Hellenistic-era confederation of Greek city states on the northern and central Peloponnese, which existed between 280 BC and 146 BC. The regional Achaean League was reformed in 281/0 BC (on the basis of a looser alliance of the founding city-states extending back to the 5th century BC), and soon expanded beyond its Achaean heartland. It was first joined by the city of Sicyon in 251, which provided it with its first great leader, Aratus of Sicyon. The League soon grew to control much of the Peloponnesus, considerably weakening the Macedonian hold on the area.
Sallust	Gaius Sallustius Crispus, generally known simply as Sallust, (86 BC - 35 BC), a Roman historian, belonged to a well-known plebeian family, and was born at Amiternum in the country of the Sabines. Throughout his career Sallust always stood by his principle as a popularis, an opposer of Pompey's party and the old aristocracy of Rome. Life and career After an ill-spent youth, Sallust entered public life and won election as Quaestor in 55 and one of the tribunes of the people in 52, the year in which the followers of Milo killed Clodius in a street brawl.
Cato the Elder	Marcus Porcius Cato (234 BC, Tusculum - 149 BC) was a Roman statesman, commonly surnamed Censorius (the Censor), Sapiens (the Wise), Priscus (the Ancient), or Major, Cato the Elder, to distinguish him from his great-grandson, Cato the Younger. He came of an ancient Plebeian family who all were noted for some military service but not for the discharge of the higher civil offices. He was bred, after the manner of his Latin forefathers, to agriculture, to which he devoted himself when not engaged in military service.
Pax Romana	Pax Romana was the long period of relative peace and minimal expansion by military force experienced by the Roman Empire in the 1st and 2nd centuries AD. Since it was established by Caesar Augustus it is sometimes called Pax Augusta. Its span was approximately 207 years (27 BC to 180 AD). Origins of the term The concept of Pax Romana was first described by Edward Gibbon in The Decline and Fall of the Roman Empire, in Chapter II. Gibbon proposed a period of moderation under Augustus and his successors and argued that generals bent on expansion were checked and recalled by the Emperors during their victories favouring consolidation ahead of further expansion.
Scipio Aemilianus	Scipio Aemilianus was a leading general and politician of the ancient Roman Republic.

Third Punic War

The Third Punic War was the third and last of the Punic Wars fought between the former Phoenician colony of Carthage, and the Roman Republic. The Punic Wars were named because of the Roman name for Carthaginians: Punici, or Poenici.

The war was a much smaller engagement than the two previous Punic Wars and primarily consisted of a single main action, the Battle of Carthage, but resulted in the complete destruction of the city of Carthage, the annexation of all remaining Carthaginian territory by Rome, and the death or enslavement of the entire Carthaginian population.

Hera

Hera was the wife and one of three sisters of Zeus in the Olympian pantheon of classical Greek Mythology. Her chief function was as the goddess of women and marriage. In Roman mythology, Juno was the equivalent mythical character.

Zeus

In Greek mythology Zeus is the 'Father of Gods and men', according to Hesiod's Theogony, who ruled the Olympians of Mount Olympus as a father ruled the family; he was the god of sky and thunder in Greek mythology. As Walter Burkert points out in his book, Greek Religion, 'Even the gods who are not his natural children address him as Father, and all the gods rise in his presence.' (Iliad, book 1.503;533). For the Greeks, he was the King of the Gods, who oversaw the universe.

Pontifex Maximus

The Pontifex Maximus was the high priest of the College of Pontiffs (Collegium Pontificum) in ancient Rome. This was the most important position in the ancient Roman religion, open only to patricians until 254 BC, when a plebeian first occupied this post. A distinctly religious office under the early Roman Republic, it gradually became politicized until, beginning with Augustus, it was subsumed into the Imperial office.

Jugurtha

Jugurtha was a King of Numidia, (Algeria), born in Cirta (modern-day Constantine).

Until the reign of Jugurtha's grandfather Masinissa, the people of Numidia were semi-nomadic and indistinguishable from the other Libyans in North Africa. Masinissa established a kingdom (roughly equivalent to modern northern Algeria) and became a Roman ally in 206 BC. After a long reign he was succeeded in 148 BC by his son Micipsa. Jugurtha, Micipsa's adopted son (and Masinissa's illegitimate grandson), was so popular among the Numidians that Micipsa was obliged to send him away to Spain.

Numidia

Numidia was an Ancient Libyan kingdom in part of present-day Algeria and Tunisia (North Africa) that later alternated between being a Roman province and being a Roman client state, and is no longer in existence today. It was located on the eastern border of modern Algeria, bordered by the Roman province of Mauretania (in modern day Algeria and Morocco) to the west, the Roman province of Africa (modern day Tunisia) to the east, the Mediterranean Sea to the north, and the Sahara Desert to the south. Its people were the Numidians.

5. The Rise of Rome, ca. 750-31B.C.E.

Teutons

The Teutons, notably Strabo and Marcus Velleius Paterculus. According to a map by Ptolemy, they originally lived in Jutland, which is in agreement with Pomponius Mela, who placed them in Scandinavia (Codanonia).

In the late 2nd century BC, many of the Teutons, under their leader Teutobod as well as the Cimbri, migrated from their original homes in southern Scandinavia and on the Jutland peninsula of Denmark, south and west to the Danube valley, where they encountered the expanding Roman Republic.

Julius Caesar

Gaius Julius Caesar was a Roman general, statesman, Consul and notable author of Latin prose. He played a critical role in the events that led to the demise of the Roman Republic and the rise of the Roman Empire. In 60 BC, Julius Caesar, Crassus and Pompey formed a political alliance that was to dominate Roman politics for several years.

Social War

The Social War, was fought from 220 BC to 217 BC between the Hellenic League under Philip V of Macedon and the Aetolian League, Sparta and Elis. It was ended with the Peace of Naupactus. Origins

Many of the tensions which led to the war were later documented by the Greek historian, Polybius.

Cisalpine Gaul

Cisalpine Gaul also called Gallia Citerior or Gallia Togata, was a Roman province until 41 BC, when it was merged into the Province of Italy. It was that part of Gallia, the land of the Gauls, which lay south and east of the Alps, as opposed to Gallia Transalpina. Its inhabitants were primarily Celtic since the expulsion of the Etruscans.

Ides of March

The Ides of March is the name of 15 March in the Roman calendar, probably referring to the day of the full moon. The term ides was used for the 15th day of the months of March, May, July, and October, and the 13th day of the other months. The Ides of March was a festive day dedicated to the god Mars and a military parade was usually held.

Second Triumvirate

The Second Triumvirate is the name historians give to the official political alliance of Octavius (later known as Augustus), Marcus Aemilius Lepidus, and Mark Antony, formed on 26 November 43 BC with the enactment of the Lex Titia, the adoption of which marked the end of the Roman Republic. The Triumvirate existed for two five-year terms, covering the period 43 BC - 33 BC.

Unlike the earlier First Triumvirate, the Second Triumvirate was an official, legally established institution, whose overwhelming power in the Roman state was given full legal sanction and whose imperium maius outranked that of all other magistrates, including the consuls.

1. Gaius _________ was a Roman general, statesman, Consul and notable author of Latin prose. He played a critical role in the events that led to the demise of the Roman Republic and the rise of the Roman Empire. In 60 BC, _________, Crassus and Pompey formed a political alliance that was to dominate Roman politics for several years.

   a. Julius Caesar
   b. Sempronia
   c. Erik the Red
   d. Synoptic Gospels

2. The _________, notably Strabo and Marcus Velleius Paterculus. According to a map by Ptolemy, they originally lived in Jutland, which is in agreement with Pomponius Mela, who placed them in Scandinavia (Codanonia).

   In the late 2nd century BC, many of the _________, under their leader Teutobod as well as the Cimbri, migrated from their original homes in southern Scandinavia and on the Jutland peninsula of Denmark, south and west to the Danube valley, where they encountered the expanding Roman Republic.

   a. Teutons
   b. Logos
   c. Local churches
   d. Synoptic Gospels

3. _________ was the long period of relative peace and minimal expansion by military force experienced by the Roman Empire in the 1st and 2nd centuries AD. Since it was established by Caesar Augustus it is sometimes called Pax Augusta. Its span was approximately 207 years (27 BC to 180 AD).

   Origins of the term

   The concept of _________ was first described by Edward Gibbon in The Decline and Fall of the Roman Empire, in Chapter II. Gibbon proposed a period of moderation under Augustus and his successors and argued that generals bent on expansion were checked and recalled by the Emperors during their victories favouring consolidation ahead of further expansion.

   a. Second Servile War
   b. Baptism of Poland
   c. Crescentii
   d. Pax Romana

4. . _________ was a leading general and politician of the ancient Roman Republic. As consul he commanded at the final siege and destruction of Carthage in 146 BC, and was a leader of the senators opposed to the Gracchi in 133 BC.

   a. Second Servile War
   b. Scipio Aemilianus
   c. Principality of Hungary

5. _________ was an Ancient Libyan kingdom in part of present-day Algeria and Tunisia (North Africa) that later alternated between being a Roman province and being a Roman client state, and is no longer in existence today. It was located on the eastern border of modern Algeria, bordered by the Roman province of Mauretania (in modern day Algeria and Morocco) to the west, the Roman province of Africa (modern day Tunisia) to the east, the Mediterranean Sea to the north, and the Sahara Desert to the south. Its people were the Numidians.

a. Numidia
b. Logos
c. Local churches
d. Synoptic Gospels

Visit Cram101.com for full Practice Exams

Visit Cram101.com for full Practice Exams

ANSWER KEY
5. The Rise of Rome, ca. 750-31B.C.E.

---

1. a

2. a

3. d

4. b

5. a

You can take the complete Chapter Practice Test

for 5. The Rise of Rome, ca. 750-31B.C.E.
on all key terms, persons, places, and concepts.

Online 99 Cents

http://www.epub141.56.21995.5.cram101.com/

Use www.Cram101.com for all your study needs

including Cram101's online interactive problem solving labs in

chemistry, statistics, mathematics, and more.

6. The Pax Romana, 31B.c.E.-284C.E.

CHAPTER OUTLINE: KEY TERMS, PEOPLE, PLACES, CONCEPTS

Pax Romana

Principate

Imperator

Punic Wars

Ab urbe condita

Ara Pacis

Caligula

Claudius

Flavian dynasty

Praetorian Guard

Year of the Four Emperors

Judaea

Colosseum

Dalmatia

Illyria

Apocalypse of Baruch

Apocalypticism

Christianity

Jesus of Nazareth

Messiah

Pontius Pilate

Dead Sea Scrolls

Essenes

Galilee

Gospel

Apostle

Church

Gospel of Thomas

Heresy

Passover

Stoicism

Eucharist

Justin Martyr

Religious persecution

Alamanni

Germanic peoples

Goths

Pax Romana

Pax Romana was the long period of relative peace and minimal expansion by military force experienced by the Roman Empire in the 1st and 2nd centuries AD. Since it was established by Caesar Augustus it is sometimes called Pax Augusta. Its span was approximately 207 years (27 BC to 180 AD).

Origins of the term

The concept of Pax Romana was first described by Edward Gibbon in The Decline and Fall of the Roman Empire, in Chapter II. Gibbon proposed a period of moderation under Augustus and his successors and argued that generals bent on expansion were checked and recalled by the Emperors during their victories favouring consolidation ahead of further expansion.

Principate

The Principate is the first period of the Roman Empire, extending from the beginning of the reign of Caesar Augustus to the Crisis of the Third Century, after which it was replaced with the Dominate. The Principate is characterized by a concerted effort on the part of the Emperors to preserve the illusion of the formal continuance of the Roman Republic.

It is etymologically derived from the Latin word princeps, meaning chief or first, the political regime dominated by such a political leader, whether or not he is formally head of state and/or head of government.

Imperator

The Latin word Imperator was a title originally roughly equivalent to commander during the period of the Roman Republic. It later went on to become a part of the titulature of the Roman Emperors as part of their cognomen. However, the Roman Emperors gained authority from a large group of titles and positions, as opposed to any single title.

Punic Wars

The Punic Wars were a series of three wars fought between Rome and Carthage from 264 B.C to 146 B.C. At the time, they were probably the largest wars that had ever taken place. The term Punic comes from the Latin word Punicus (or Poenicus), meaning 'Carthaginian', with reference to the Carthaginians' Phoenician ancestry.

Ab urbe condita

Ab urbe condita. is Latin for 'from the founding of the City (Rome)', traditionally set in 753 BC. Ab urbe condita is a year-numbering system used by some ancient Roman historians to identify particular Roman years. Renaissance editors sometimes added Ab urbe condita to Roman manuscripts they published, giving the false impression that the Romans usually numbered their years using the Ab urbe condita system.

Ara Pacis

The Ara Pacis Augustae is an altar to Peace, envisioned as a Roman goddess. It was commissioned by the Roman Senate on 4 July 13 BC to honor the triumphal return from Hispania and Gaul of the Roman emperor Augustus, and was consecrated on 30 January 9 BC by the Senate to celebrate the peace established in the Empire after Augustus's victories.

6. The Pax Romana, 31B.c.E.-284C.E.

Caligula

Caligula was Roman Emperor from 37 to 41. Caligula was a member of the house of rulers conventionally known as the Julio-Claudian dynasty. Caligula's father Germanicus, the nephew and adopted son of emperor Tiberius, was a very successful general and one of Rome's most beloved public figures. The young Gaius earned the nickname Caligula (meaning 'little soldier's boot', the diminutive form of caliga, n. hob-nailed military boot) from his father's soldiers while accompanying him during his campaigns in Germania. When Germanicus died at Antioch in 19 AD, his wife Agrippina the Elder returned to Rome with her six children where she became entangled in an increasingly bitter feud with Tiberius. This conflict eventually led to the destruction of her family, with Caligula as the sole male survivor. Unscathed by the deadly intrigues, Caligula accepted the invitation to join the emperor on the island of Capri in 31, where Tiberius himself had withdrawn five years earlier. At the death of Tiberius in 37, Caligula succeeded his great-uncle and adoptive grandfather.

Claudius

Tiberius Claudius Caesar Augustus Germanicus (1 August 10 BC - 13 October AD 54), born Tiberius Claudius Drusus, then Tiberius Claudius Nero Germanicus until his accession, was Roman Emperor from 41 to 54 AD. A member of the Julio-Claudian dynasty, he was the son of Drusus and Antonia Minor. He was born at Lugdunum in Gaul and was the first emperor to be born outside Italy. Afflicted with a limp and slight deafness due to sickness at a young age, his family ostracized him and excluded him from public office until his consulship with his nephew Caligula in 37 AD. Claudius' infirmity probably saved him from the fate of many other nobles during the purges of Tiberius' and Caligula's reigns; potential enemies did not see him as a serious threat.

Flavian dynasty

The Flavian dynasty was a Roman Imperial Dynasty, which ruled the Roman Empire between 69 and 96 AD, encompassing the reigns of Vespasian (69-79), and his two sons Titus (79-81) and Domitian (81-96). The Flavians rose to power during the civil war of 69, known as the Year of the Four Emperors. After Galba and Otho died in quick succession, Vitellius became emperor in mid 69. His claim to the throne was quickly challenged by legions stationed in the Eastern provinces, who declared their commander Vespasian Emperor in his place.

Praetorian Guard

The Praetorian Guard was a force of bodyguards used by Roman Emperors. The title was already used during the Roman Republic for the guards of Roman generals, at least since the rise to prominence of the Scipio family around 275 BC. The Guard was dissolved by Emperor Constantine I in the 4th century.

History

The term Praetorian derived from the tent of the commanding general or praetor of a Roman army in the field--the praetorium.

Year of the Four Emperors

The Year of the Four Emperors was a year in the history of the Roman Empire, AD 69, in which four emperors ruled in a remarkable succession. These four emperors were Galba, Otho, Vitellius, and Vespasian.

The suicide of emperor Nero, in 68, was followed by a brief period of civil war, the first Roman civil war since Mark Antony's death in 30 BC. Between June 68 and December of 69, Rome witnessed the successive rise and fall of Galba, Otho and Vitellius until the final accession of Vespasian, first ruler of the Flavian Dynasty, in July 69. This period of civil war has become emblematic of the cyclic political disturbances in the history of the Roman Empire.

Judaea

Judaea is the term used by historians to refer to the Roman province that extended over parts of the former regions of the Hasmonean and Herodian kingdoms of Israel. It was named after Herod Archelaus's ethnarchy of Judea of which it was an expansion, the latter name deriving from the Kingdom of Judah of the 6th century BCE.

Rome's involvement in the area dated from 63 BCE, following the end of the Third Mithridatic War, when Rome made Syria a province. After the defeat of Mithridates VI of Pontus, general Pompeius Magnus (Pompey the Great) remained to secure the area.

Colosseum

The Colosseum, originally the Flavian Amphitheatre, is an elliptical amphitheatre in the centre of the city of Rome, Italy, the largest ever built in the Roman Empire. It is considered one of the greatest works of Roman architecture and Roman engineering.

Occupying a site just east of the Roman Forum, its construction started in 72 AD under the emperor Vespasian and was completed in 80 AD under Titus, with further modifications being made during Domitian's reign (81-96).

Dalmatia

The Theme of Dalmatia was a Byzantine theme (a military-civilian province) on the eastern coast of the Adriatic Sea in Southeastern Europe, headquartered at Zadar. Origins

Dalmatia first came under Byzantine control in the 530s, when the generals of Emperor Justinian I (r. 527-565) seized it from the Ostrogoths in the Gothic War. The invasions of the Avars and Slavs in the 7th century destroyed the main cities and overran much of the hinterland, with Byzantine control limited to the islands and certain new coastal cities such as Split and Dubrovnik, while Zara (Zadar) became the local episcopal and administrative center, under an archon.

Illyria

In classical antiquity, Illyria was a region in the western part of the Balkan Peninsula inhabited by the Illyrians.

The prehistory of Illyria and the Illyrians is known from archaeological evidence. The Romans conquered the region in 168 BC in the aftermath of the Illyrian Wars.

6. The Pax Romana, 31B.c.E.-284C.E.

CHAPTER HIGHLIGHTS & NOTES: KEY TERMS, PEOPLE, PLACES, CONCEPTS

Apocalypticism	Apocalypticism is the religious belief that there will be an apocalypse, a term which originally referred to a revelation of God's will, but now usually refers to belief that the world will come to an end time very soon, even within one's own lifetime. This belief is usually accompanied by the idea that civilization, as we know it, will soon come to a tumultuous end with some sort of catastrophic global event such as war. Apocalypticism is often conjoined with esoteric knowledge that will likely be revealed in a major confrontation between good and evil forces, destined to change the course of history.
Christianity	Christianity is a monotheistic and Abrahamic religion based on the life and teachings of Jesus Christ as presented in canonical gospels and other New Testament writings. Most adherents of the Christian faith, known as Christians, believe that Jesus is the Son of God, fully divine and fully human and the savior of humanity prophesied in the Old Testament. Consequentially, Christians commonly refer to Jesus as Christ or Messiah.
Jesus of Nazareth	Jesus of Nazareth is the first volume in Pope Benedict XVI's planned three-volume meditation on the life and teachings of Jesus Christ. The first book authored by Benedict since his ascension to the papacy, it was published by Doubleday in 2007. In the book's introduction, the pope explicitly states that the treatise is in 'no way an exercise of the magisterium,' but rather an 'expression of his personal search for the face of the Lord.' Jesus of Nazareth's ten chapters cover the bulk of Jesus' public ministry, encompassing subjects and events such as Christ's baptism at the hands of John the Baptist, the Sermon on the Mount, the meaning of the parables, the Calling of the Twelve, the Confession of Peter, and the Transfiguration.
Messiah	Messiah, designates a king or High Priest traditionally anointed with holy anointing oil as described in Exodus 30:22-25. The term was not applied exclusively to Jewish kings, and the Hebrew Bible refers to Cyrus the Great, king of Persia, as a messiah. Following the death of Simon bar Kokhba, the term came to refer to a Jewish king who would rule at the end of history. In later Jewish messianic tradition and eschatology, messiah refers to a leader anointed by God, and in some cases, a future King of Israel, physically descended from the Davidic line, who will rule the united tribes of Israel and herald the Messianic Age of global peace.
Pontius Pilate	Pontius Pilate was the fifth Prefect of the Roman province of Judaea, from AD 26-36. He is best known as the judge at Jesus' trial and the man who authorized the Crucifixion of Jesus. Pilate appears in all four Canonical gospels in association with the responsibility for the death of Jesus. In Matthew, Pilate washes his hands of Jesus and reluctantly sends him to his death.
Dead Sea Scrolls	The Dead Sea Scrolls are a collection of 972 texts discovered between 1946 and 1956 at Khirbet Qumran in what was then British Mandate Palestine, and since 1947 known as the West Bank.

They were found on the northwest shore of the Dead Sea, from which they derive their name. The texts are of great historical, religious and linguistic significance because they include the earliest known surviving manuscripts of works later included in the Hebrew Bible canon, along with extra-biblical manuscripts which preserve evidence of the diversity of religious thought in late Second Temple Judaism.

Essenes

The Essenes were a sect of Second Temple Judaism that flourished from the 2nd century BCE to the 1st century CE which some scholars claim seceded from the Zadokite priests. Being much fewer in number than the Pharisees and the Sadducees (the other two major sects at the time), the Essenes lived in various cities but congregated in communal life dedicated to asceticism, voluntary poverty, daily immersion, and abstinence from worldly pleasures, including (for some groups) celibacy. Many separate but related religious groups of that era shared similar mystic, eschatological, messianic, and ascetic beliefs.

Galilee

Galilee, is a large region in northern Israel which overlaps with much of the administrative North District of the country. Traditionally divided into Upper Galilee, Lower Galilee, and Western Galilee, extending from Dan to the north, at the base of Mount Hermon, along Mount Lebanon to the ridges of Mount Carmel and Mount Gilboa to the south, and from the Jordan Rift Valley to the east across the plains of the Jezreel Valley and Acre to the shores of the Mediterranean Sea and the Coastal Plain in the west.

Most of Galilee consists of rocky terrain, at heights of between 500 and 700 metres.

Gospel

The Gospel in Christian liturgy refers to a reading from the Gospels used during various religious services, including Mass or Divine Liturgy (Eucharist). In many Christian churches, all present stand when a passage from one of the Gospels is read publicly, and sit when a passage from a different part of the Bible is read. The reading of the Gospels, often contained in a liturgical edition containing only the four Gospels , is traditionally done by a minister, priest or deacon, and in many traditions the Gospel Book is brought into the midst of the congregation to be read.

Apostle

The term apostle is derived from Classical Greek ?π?στολος (apóstolos), meaning 'one who is sent away', from στ?λλω ('stello', 'send') + απ? (apo, 'away from'). The literal meaning in English is therefore an 'emissary', from the Latin mitto ('send') and ex ('from'). The purpose of such 'sending away' is to convey messages.

Church

In the Christian religion, a church is a building or structure to facilitate the meeting of its members. Originally, Jewish Christians met in synagogues, such as the Cenacle, and in one another's homes, known as house churches. As Christianity grew and became more accepted by governments, notably with the Edict of Milan, rooms and, eventually, entire buildings were set aside for the explicit purpose of Christian worship, such as the Church of the Holy Sepulcher.

Visit Cram101.com for full Practice Exams

Gospel of Thomas	The Gospel According to Thomas, commonly shortened to the Gospel of Thomas, is a well preserved early Christian, non-canonical sayings-gospel discovered near Nag Hammadi, Egypt, in December 1945, in one of a group of books known as the Nag Hammadi library. The Coptic language text, the second of seven contained in what modern-day scholars have designated as Codex II, is composed of 114 sayings attributed to Jesus. Almost half of these sayings resemble those found in the Canonical Gospels, while the other sayings were previously unknown.
Heresy	Heresy is a controversial or novel change to a system of beliefs, especially a religion, that conflicts with established dogma. It is distinct from apostasy, which is the formal denunciation of one's religion, principles or cause, and blasphemy, which is irreverence toward religion. The founder or leader of a heretical movement is called a heresiarch, while individuals who espouse heresy or commit heresy, are known as heretics.
Passover	Christian Passover is a religious observance celebrated by some churches to keep faith with Old Testament teaching. It is often linked to the Christian holiday and festival of Easter. Often, only an abbreviated seder is celebrated to explain the meaning in a time-limited ceremony.
Stoicism	Stoicism is a school of Hellenistic philosophy founded in Athens by Zeno of Citium in the early 3rd century BC. The Stoics taught that destructive emotions resulted from errors in judgment, and that a sage, or person of 'moral and intellectual perfection,' would not suffer such emotions. Stoics were concerned with the active relationship between cosmic determinism and human freedom, and the belief that it is virtuous to maintain a will (called prohairesis) that is in accord with nature. Because of this, the Stoics presented their philosophy as a way of life, and they thought that the best indication of an individual's philosophy was not what a person said but how he behaved.
Eucharist	The Eucharist, Sacrament of the Altar, the Blessed Sacrament, or The Lord's Supper, and other names, is a Christian sacrament or ordinance, generally considered to be a re-enactment of the Last Supper, the final meal that Jesus Christ shared with his disciples before his arrest and crucifixion, during which he gave them bread, saying, 'This is my body', and wine, saying, 'This is my blood'. There are different interpretations of the significance of the Eucharist, but 'there is more of a consensus among Christians about the meaning of the Eucharist than would appear from the confessional debates over the sacramental presence, the effects of the Eucharist, and the proper auspices under which it may be celebrated.'

Visit Cram101.com for full Practice Exams

The phrase 'the Eucharist' may refer not only to the rite but also to the consecrated bread (leavened or unleavened) and wine or, unfermented grape juice (in some Protestant denominations) or water (in Mormonism), used in the rite, and, in this sense, communicants may speak of 'receiving the Eucharist', as well as 'celebrating the Eucharist'.

Names and their origin

Eucharist, from Greek ε?χαριστ?α (eucharistia), means 'thanksgiving'.

Justin Martyr

Justin Martyr, also known as just Saint Justin (AD 100-ca.165), was an early Christian apologist, and is regarded as the foremost interpreter of the theory of the Logos in the 2nd century. Most of his works are lost, but two apologies and a dialogue did survive. He is considered a saint by the Roman Catholic Church, the Anglican Church, and the Eastern Orthodox Church.

Religious persecution

Religious persecution is the systematic mistreatment of an individual or group of individuals as a response to their religious beliefs or affiliations or lack thereof.

The tendency of societies or groups within society to alienate or repress different subcultures is a recurrent theme in human history. Moreover, because a person's religion often determines to a significant extent his or her morality and personal identity, religious differences can be significant cultural factors.

Alamanni

The Alamanni, Allemanni, or Alemanni were originally an alliance of Germanic tribes located around the upper Rhine river . One of the earliest references to them is the cognomen Alamannicus assumed by Roman Emperor Caracalla, who ruled the Roman Empire from 211 to 217 and claimed thereby to be their conqueror. The nature of this alliance and their previous tribal affiliations remain uncertain.

Germanic peoples

The Germanic peoples are a historical ethno-linguistic group, originating in Northern Europe and identified by their use of the Indo-European Germanic languages, which diversified out of Common Germanic in the course of the Pre-Roman Iron Age. The descendants of these peoples became, and in many areas contributed to, ethnic groups in North Western Europe: Scandinavians (Danes, Swedes, Norwegians, Icelanders, and Faroe Islanders, but not Finns and Sami), Germans, Dutch, Flemish, and English, among others.

Migrating Germanic peoples spread throughout Europe in Late Antiquity (300-600) and the Early Middle Ages.

Goths

The Goths were an East Germanic people, two of whose branches, the Visigoths and the Ostrogoths, played an important role in the fall of the Roman Empire and the emergence of Medieval Europe.

6. The Pax Romana, 31B.c.E.-284C.E.

CHAPTER HIGHLIGHTS & NOTES: KEY TERMS, PEOPLE, PLACES, CONCEPTS

An important source of our knowledge of the Goths is Getica, a semi-fictional account, written in the sixth century by the Roman historian Jordanes, of their migration from southern Scandza (Scandinavia), into Gothiscandza-believed to be the lower Vistula region in modern Pomerania-and from there to the coast of the Black Sea. Archaeological evidence from the Pomeranian Wielbark culture and the Chernyakhov culture, northeast of the lower Danube, confirms that some such migration did in fact take place.

CHAPTER QUIZ: KEY TERMS, PEOPLE, PLACES, CONCEPTS

1. _________ was the long period of relative peace and minimal expansion by military force experienced by the Roman Empire in the 1st and 2nd centuries AD. Since it was established by Caesar Augustus it is sometimes called Pax Augusta. Its span was approximately 207 years (27 BC to 180 AD).

   Origins of the term

   The concept of _________ was first described by Edward Gibbon in The Decline and Fall of the Roman Empire, in Chapter II. Gibbon proposed a period of moderation under Augustus and his successors and argued that generals bent on expansion were checked and recalled by the Emperors during their victories favouring consolidation ahead of further expansion.

   a. Pax Romana
   b. Baptism of Poland
   c. Crescentii
   d. History of Christianity in Ukraine

2. _________, is a large region in northern Israel which overlaps with much of the administrative North District of the country. Traditionally divided into Upper _________, Lower _________, and Western _________, extending from Dan to the north, at the base of Mount Hermon, along Mount Lebanon to the ridges of Mount Carmel and Mount Gilboa to the south, and from the Jordan Rift Valley to the east across the plains of the Jezreel Valley and Acre to the shores of the Mediterranean Sea and the Coastal Plain in the west.

   Most of _________ consists of rocky terrain, at heights of between 500 and 700 metres.

   a. Galilee
   b. The Jesus Dynasty
   c. Jesus before Christianity
   d. Nicolas Notovitch

3. The _________ is the first period of the Roman Empire, extending from the beginning of the reign of Caesar Augustus to the Crisis of the Third Century, after which it was replaced with the Dominate. The _________ is characterized by a concerted effort on the part of the Emperors to preserve the illusion of the formal continuance of the Roman Republic.

   It is etymologically derived from the Latin word princeps, meaning chief or first, the political regime dominated by such a political leader, whether or not he is formally head of state and/or head of government.

   a. Principate
   b. Quinquegentiani
   c. Roman dodecahedron
   d. Roman Emperors Route

4. The Theme of _________ was a Byzantine theme (a military-civilian province) on the eastern coast of the Adriatic Sea in Southeastern Europe, headquartered at Zadar. Origins

   _________ first came under Byzantine control in the 530s, when the generals of Emperor Justinian I (r. 527-565) seized it from the Ostrogoths in the Gothic War. The invasions of the Avars and Slavs in the 7th century destroyed the main cities and overran much of the hinterland, with Byzantine control limited to the islands and certain new coastal cities such as Split and Dubrovnik, while Zara (Zadar) became the local episcopal and administrative center, under an archon.

   a. Governorate of Dalmatia
   b. Kingdom of Dalmatia
   c. Dalmatian Action
   d. Dalmatia

5. The _________, originally the Flavian Amphitheatre, is an elliptical amphitheatre in the centre of the city of Rome, Italy, the largest ever built in the Roman Empire. It is considered one of the greatest works of Roman architecture and Roman engineering.

   Occupying a site just east of the Roman Forum, its construction started in 72 AD under the emperor Vespasian and was completed in 80 AD under Titus, with further modifications being made during Domitian's reign (81-96).

   a. Flavian Amphitheater
   b. Trajan's Market
   c. Colosseum
   d. Second Servile War

Visit Cram101.com for full Practice Exams

ANSWER KEY

6. The Pax Romana, 31B.c.E.-284C.E.

1. a

2. a

3. a

4. d

5. c

You can take the complete Chapter Practice Test

for 6. The Pax Romana, 31B.c.E.-284C.E.

on all key terms, persons, places, and concepts.

Online 99 Cents

http://www.epub141.56.21995.6.cram101.com/

Use www.Cram101.com for all your study needs

including Cram101's online interactive problem solving labs in

chemistry, statistics, mathematics, and more.

7. Late Antiquity, 250-600

CHAPTER OUTLINE: KEY TERMS, PEOPLE, PLACES, CONCEPTS

Late Antiquity

Byzantine Empire

Christianity

Religious persecution

Arianism

Arius

Nicene Creed

Canon law

Holy Spirit

Canon

Apostolic succession

Bishop

Christian Church

Christian monasticism

Church

Rule of Saint Benedict

Mary Magdalene

Garden of Eden

Original sin

Barbarian

Society

7. Late Antiquity, 250-600

CHAPTER OUTLINE: KEY TERMS, PEOPLE, PLACES, CONCEPTS

- Burgundian
- Ostrogoths
- Salian Franks
- Salic law
- Huns
- Gauls
- Germanic peoples
- Picts
- Viking
- Attila
- Goths
- Valens
- Vandals
- Merovech
- Merovingian dynasty
- Justinian
- Lombards
- Christianization
- Martin of Tours
- Canterbury
- Synod of Whitby

7. Late Antiquity, 250-600

CHAPTER OUTLINE: KEY TERMS, PEOPLE, PLACES, CONCEPTS

_______________	Conversion to Christianity
_______________	Jurisprudence
_______________	Bubonic plague
_______________	Cyrillic alphabet
_______________	Orthodox Christianity
_______________	Secret History
_______________	Third Rome

CHAPTER HIGHLIGHTS & NOTES: KEY TERMS, PEOPLE, PLACES, CONCEPTS

Late Antiquity	Late Antiquity is a periodization used by historians to describe the time of transition from Classical Antiquity to the Middle Ages, in both mainland Europe and the Mediterranean world. Precise boundaries for the period are a matter of debate, but historian of the period Peter Brown proposed a period between the 2nd and 8th centuries. Generally, it can be thought of as from the end of the Roman Empire's Crisis of the Third Century (c. 235 - 284) to the re-organization of the Eastern Roman Empire under Heraclius and the Muslim conquests in the mid-7th century.
Byzantine Empire	The Byzantine Empire is a term used by modern historians to distinguish the Constantinople-centred Roman Empire of the Middle Ages from its earlier classical existence. It is also referred to as the Eastern Roman Empire, primarily in the context of Late Antiquity, while the Empire was still administered with separate eastern and western political centres. Its citizens continued to refer to their empire as the Roman Empire or Romania .
Christianity	Christianity is a monotheistic and Abrahamic religion based on the life and teachings of Jesus Christ as presented in canonical gospels and other New Testament writings. Most adherents of the Christian faith, known as Christians, believe that Jesus is the Son of God, fully divine and fully human and the savior of humanity prophesied in the Old Testament. Consequentially, Christians commonly refer to Jesus as Christ or Messiah.
Religious persecution	Religious persecution is the systematic mistreatment of an individual or group of individuals as a response to their religious beliefs or affiliations or lack thereof.

The tendency of societies or groups within society to alienate or repress different subcultures is a recurrent theme in human history. Moreover, because a person's religion often determines to a significant extent his or her morality and personal identity, religious differences can be significant cultural factors.

Arianism

Arianism is the theological teaching attributed to Arius (ca. AD 250-336), a Christian presbyter from Alexandria, Egypt, concerning the relationship of the entities of the Trinity ('God the Father', 'God the Son' and 'God the Holy Spirit') and the precise nature of the Son of God. The Roman Emperors Constantius II (337-361) and Valens (364-378) were Arians or Semi-Arians. The Arian concept of Christ is that the Son of God did not always exist, but was created by--and is therefore distinct from and inferior to--God the Father.

Arius

Arius was a Christian presbyter from Alexandria, Egypt. His teachings about the nature of the Godhead, which emphasized the Father's Divinity over the Son, and his opposition to the Athanasian or Trinitarian Christology, made him a controversial figure in the First Council of Nicea, convened by Roman Emperor Constantine in AD 325. After Emperor Constantine legalized and formalized the Christianity of the time in the Roman Empire, the newly recognized Catholic Church sought to unify and clarify its theology. Trinitarian partisans, including Athanasius, used Arius and Arianism as epithets to describe those who disagreed with their doctrine of co-equal Trinitarianism, a Christology representing the Father and Son (Jesus of Nazareth) as 'of one essence' (consubstantial) and coeternal.

Nicene Creed

The Nicene Creed is the creed or profession of faith that is most widely used in Christian liturgy. It is called Nicene ( ) because, in its original form, it was adopted in the city of Nicaea by the first ecumenical council, which met there in the year 325.

The Nicene Creed has been normative for the Anglican Church, the Church of the East, the Eastern Orthodox Church, the Oriental Orthodox churches, the Roman Catholic Church including the Eastern Catholic Churches, the Old Catholic Church, the Lutheran Church and many Protestant denominations, forming the eponymous mainstream definition of Christianity itself in Nicene Christianity.

Canon law

The canon law of the Catholic Church is a fully developed legal system, with all the necessary elements: courts, lawyers, judges, a fully articulated legal code and principles of legal interpretation. It lacks the necessary binding force present in most modern day legal systems. The academic degrees in canon law are the J.C.B. (Juris Canonici Baccalaureatus, Bachelor of Canon Law, normally taken as a graduate degree), J.C.L. (Juris Canonici Licentiatus, Licentiate of Canon Law) and the J.C.D. (Juris Canonici Doctor, Doctor of Canon Law).

Holy Spirit

Holy Spirit is a term found in English translations of the Bible, but understood differently among the Abrahamic religions.

While the general concept of a 'Spirit' that permeates the cosmos is a general feature of most religions (e.g. Brahman in Hinduism and Tao in Taoism and Great Spirit among Indigenous peoples of the Americas), the term Holy Spirit specifically refers to the beliefs held in the Abrahamic religions.

For the majority of Christians, the belief in the Holy Trinity implies the existence of three distinct Holy Persons: God the Father, God the Son and God the Holy Spirit being One Eternal Triune God.

Canon

A canon is a structured hymn used in a number of Eastern Orthodox services. It consists of nine odes, sometimes called canticles or songs depending on the translation, based on the Biblical canticles. Most of these are found in the Old Testament, but the final ode is taken from the Magnificat and Song of Zechariah from the New Testament.

Apostolic succession

Apostolic succession is 'the method whereby the ministry of the Christian Church is held to be derived from the apostles by a continuous succession' which is usually located in a series of bishops who have succeeded one another in the same see. It derived its origin directly from one of the apostles or indirectly through the initiative of an apostolic see. Bishops are seen not as succeeding to the apostolic office itself and being themselves apostles, but instead as succeeding to the pastoral care of the Christian community founded by the apostles.

Bishop

In the Catholic Church, a bishop is an ordained minister who holds the fullness of the sacrament of Holy Orders and is responsible for teaching doctrine, governing Catholics in his jurisdiction, and sanctifying the world and for representing the Church. Catholics trace the origins of the office of bishop to the apostles, who were endowed with a special charism by the Holy Spirit at Pentecost. Catholics believe this special charism has been transmitted through an unbroken succession of bishops by the laying on of hands in the sacrament of Holy Orders.

Christian Church

The Christian Church is the assembly or association of followers of Jesus Christ. The Greek term ? κκλησ?α, which in its appearances in the New Testament is usually translated as 'church', basically means 'assembly'. The term appears in two verses of the canonical Gospel of Matthew, twenty-four verses of the Acts of the Apostles, fifty-eight verses of the letters of Paul the Apostle (including the earliest instances of its use in relation to a Christian body), two verses of the Letter to the Hebrews, one verse of the Epistle of James, three verses of the Third Epistle of John, and nineteen verses of the Book of Revelation.

Christian monasticism

Christian monasticism is a practice which began to develop early in the history of the Christian Church, modeled upon scriptural examples and ideals, including those in the Old Testament, but not mandated as an institution in the scriptures. It has come to be regulated by religious rules and, in modern times, the Canon law of the respective Christian denominations that have forms of monastic living.

Church	In the Christian religion, a church is a building or structure to facilitate the meeting of its members. Originally, Jewish Christians met in synagogues, such as the Cenacle, and in one another's homes, known as house churches. As Christianity grew and became more accepted by governments, notably with the Edict of Milan, rooms and, eventually, entire buildings were set aside for the explicit purpose of Christian worship, such as the Church of the Holy Sepulcher.
Rule of Saint Benedict	The Rule of Saint Benedict is a book of precepts written by St. Benedict of Nursia (c.480-547) for monks living communally under the authority of an abbot. Since about the 7th century it has also been adopted by communities of women. During the 1500 years of its existence, it has become the leading guide in Western Christianity for monastic living in community.
Mary Magdalene	Mary Magdalene is described, in the New Testament, as one of the most important women associated with Jesus during his ministry. The late 20th and early 21st century has seen a restoration of the New Testament figure of Mary Magdalene as a patron of women's preaching and ministry. Her new popularity has stemmed in part from the recognition that Mary Magdalene has suffered from what is believed to have been a historical defamation of character.
Garden of Eden	The Garden of Eden is described in the Book of Genesis as being the place where the first man, Adam, and his wife, Eve, lived after they were created by God. Literally, the Bible speaks about a garden in Eden (Gen. 2:8). This garden forms part of the Genesis creation narrative and theodicy of the Abrahamic religions, often being used to explain the origin of sin and mankind's wrongdoings.
Original sin	Original sin, is, according to a doctrine proposed in Christian theology, humanity's state of sin resulting from the Fall of Man. This condition has been characterized in many ways, ranging from something as insignificant as a slight deficiency, or a tendency toward sin yet without collective guilt, referred to as a 'sin nature,' to something as drastic as total depravity or automatic guilt by all humans through collective guilt. Those who uphold this doctrine look to the teaching of Paul the Apostle in Romans 5:12-21 and 1 Corinthians 15:22 for its scriptural base, and see it as perhaps implied in an Old Testament passage Psalm 51:5.
Barbarian	Barbarian and Savage are pejorative terms used to refer to a person who is perceived to be uncivilized. The word is often used either in a general reference to a member of a nation or ethnos, typically a tribal society as seen by an urban civilization either viewed as inferior, or admired as a noble savage. In idiomatic or figurative usage, a 'barbarian' may also be an individual reference to a brutal, cruel, warlike, insensitive person.

7. Late Antiquity, 250-600

Society

A society, is a group of people related to each other through persistent relations, or a large social grouping sharing the same geographical or virtual territory, subject to the same political authority and dominant cultural expectations. Human societies are characterized by patterns of relationships (social relations) between individuals who share a distinctive culture and institutions; a given society may be described as the sum total of such relationships among its constituent members. In the social sciences, a larger society often evinces stratification and/or dominance patterns in subgroups.

Burgundian

The Burgundian party was a political allegiance in France that formed during the reign of Charles VI during the latter half of the Hundred Years' War. During that era the term 'Burgundian' also applied to loyal subjects of the dukes of Burgundy.

The Dukes of Burgundy had inherited a large number of lands scattered from what is now the border of Switzerland up to the North Sea.

Ostrogoths

The Ostrogoths were a branch of the later Goths (the other major branch being the Visigoths). The Ostrogoths, under Theoderic the Great, established a kingdom in Italy in the late 5th and 6th centuries. The Ostrogoths traced their origins to the Greutungi and a semi-legendary kingdom north of the Black Sea in the 3rd and 4th centuries.

Salian Franks

The Salian Franks or Salii were a subgroup of the early Franks who originally had been living north of the limes in the area north of the Rhine. The Merovingian kings responsible for the conquest of Gaul were Salians. From the 3rd century on, the Salian Franks appear in the historical records as warlike Germanic people and pirates, and as Laeti (allies of the Romans).

Salic law

Salic law, or Salian Law, was the major body of Frankish law governing all the Franks of Frankia under the rule of its kings during the Old Frankish Period, approximately equal to the early Middle Ages. The laws were maintained in written form in the Latin language by a committee empowered by the monarch. Dozens of manuscripts dated from the 8th century of a putative original recension in the 6th century and three emendations as late as the 9th century have survived.

Huns

The Huns were a group of nomadic people who first appeared in Europe from east of the Volga River, region of the earlier Scythians, with a migration intertwined with the Alans. They were first mentioned as Hunnoi by Tacitus. Initially being near the Caspian Sea in 91 AD, the Huns migrated to the southeastern area of the Caucasus by about 150 AD and into Europe by 370 AD, where they established a vast Hunnic Empire.

Gauls

The Gauls were a Celtic people living in Gaul, the region roughly corresponding to what is now France, Belgium, Switzerland and Northern Italy, from the Iron Age through the Roman period. They mostly spoke the Continental Celtic language called Gaulish.

Gauls under Brennus defeated Roman forces in a battle circa 390 BCE.

Germanic peoples

The Germanic peoples are a historical ethno-linguistic group, originating in Northern Europe and identified by their use of the Indo-European Germanic languages, which diversified out of Common Germanic in the course of the Pre-Roman Iron Age. The descendants of these peoples became, and in many areas contributed to, ethnic groups in North Western Europe: Scandinavians (Danes, Swedes, Norwegians, Icelanders, and Faroe Islanders, but not Finns and Sami), Germans, Dutch, Flemish, and English, among others.

Migrating Germanic peoples spread throughout Europe in Late Antiquity (300-600) and the Early Middle Ages.

Picts

The Picts were a group of Late Iron Age and Early Mediaeval Celtic people living in ancient eastern and northern Scotland. There is an association with the distribution of brochs, place names beginning 'Pit-', for instance Pitlochry, and Pictish stones. They are recorded from before the Roman conquest of Britain until the 10th century, when they merged with the Gaels.

Viking

Viking is the name of the son of Vífil and Eimyrja in Þorsteins saga Víkingssonar. Viking is the father of Thorsten and Thorer.

The two daughters of Logi (Haloge) were stolen away by suitors to nearby islands.

Attila

Attila (also known as Attila the Hun in the UK) was an American TV miniseries set during the waning days of the Western Roman Empire, in particular during the invasions of the Huns in Europe.

The miniseries tells the story of one of the most ferocious warriors in the world, Attila the Hun, who violently assumes Hun leadership and unites the warring clans under his banner. Cast •Gerard Butler - Attila•Powers Boothe - Flavius Aetius•Simmone Jade Mackinnon - N'Kara/Ildico•Reg Rogers - Valentinian III•Alice Krige - Placidia•Pauline Lynch - Galen•Steven Berkoff - Rua•Andrew Pleavin - Orestes•Tommy Flanagan - Bleda•Kirsty Mitchell - Honoria•Jonathan Hyde - Flavius Felix•Tim Curry - Theodosius II•Janet Henfrey - Palcharia•Liam Cunningham - Theodoric I•Rollo Weeks - Young Attila•Richard Lumsden - Petronius•Mark Letheren - Thorismund•Jolyon Baker - Mundzuk•David Bailie - The ShamanHistorical Inaccuracies •There is no evidence that Attila ever spent time in Rome, although Aetius was a hostage for a time among the Huns.•The Romans are portrayed in standard Hollywood terms, decadent pagan orgies and all - whereas in reality by this stage they had converted to a particularly stern and moralistic Christianity.•The film depicts the Battle of Chalons as the last major campaign of Attila's career, entirely omitting his campaign the following year in Italy, during which he very nearly sacked Rome but withdrew after meeting with the Pope and Roman officials.•Attila's first wife, N'kara, is entirely fictional as is the daughter of Aetius/Theodoric - although the fact that Attila had adult sons by his death does suggest that he had been married before - perhaps many times.

7. Late Antiquity, 250-600

Goths

The Goths were an East Germanic people, two of whose branches, the Visigoths and the Ostrogoths, played an important role in the fall of the Roman Empire and the emergence of Medieval Europe.

An important source of our knowledge of the Goths is Getica, a semi-fictional account, written in the sixth century by the Roman historian Jordanes, of their migration from southern Scandza (Scandinavia), into Gothiscandza-believed to be the lower Vistula region in modern Pomerania-and from there to the coast of the Black Sea. Archaeological evidence from the Pomeranian Wielbark culture and the Chernyakhov culture, northeast of the lower Danube, confirms that some such migration did in fact take place.

Valens

Valens was the Eastern Roman Emperor from 364 to 378. He was given the eastern half of the empire by his brother Valentinian I after the latter's accession to the throne. Valens, sometimes known as the Last True Roman, was defeated and killed in the Battle of Adrianople, which marked the beginning of the fall of the Western Roman Empire.

Vandals

The Vandals were an East Germanic tribe who in 429 under king Genseric entered Africa and by 439 established a kingdom which included the Roman Africa province, besides the islands of Sicily, Corsica, Sardinia, Malta and the Balearics. In 455, they sacked the city of Rome. Their kingdom collapsed in the Vandalic War of 533-4, in which Justinian I managed to reconquer the Africa province for the Eastern Roman (Byzantine) Empire.

Merovech

Merovech is the semi-legendary founder of the Merovingian dynasty of the Salian Franks (although Chlodio may in fact be the founder), which later became the dominant Frankish tribe. He allegedly lived in the first half of the fifth century.

Merovingian dynasty

The Merovingians were a Salian Frankish dynasty that came to rule the Franks in a region known as Francia in Latin for 300 years from the middle of the 5th century, their territory largely corresponding to ancient Gaul as well as the Roman provinces of Raetia, Germania Superior and the southern part of Germania Magna. The Merovingian dynasty was founded by Childeric I (c.457 - 481) the son of Merovech, leader of the Salian Franks, but it was his famous son Clovis I (481 - 511) who united all of Gaul under Merovingian rule.

After the death of Clovis there were frequent clashes between different branches of the family, but when threatened by its neighbours the Merovingians presented a strong united front.

Justinian

Justinian (ISBN 0-8125-4527-3), was published in 1998 by Tor Books. It is a novel by American writer Harry Turtledove writing under the pseudonym H. N. Turteltaub, a name he uses when writing historical fiction.

Lombards	The Lombards, were a Germanic tribe who ruled a Kingdom in Italy from 568 to 774. The Lombard historian Paul the Deacon wrote in the Historia Langobardorum that the Lombards descended from a small tribe called the Winnili who dwelt in southern Scandinavia (Scadanan) before migrating to seek new lands. In the 1st century AD they formed part of the Suebi, in northwestern Germany.
Christianization	The historical phenomenon of Christianization is the conversion of individuals to Christianity or the conversion of entire peoples at once. It also includes the practice of converting native pagan practices and culture, pagan religious imagery, pagan sites and the pagan calendar to Christian uses, due to the Christian efforts at proselytism (evangelism) based on the tradition of the Great Commission. Various strategies and techniques were employed in Christianization campaigns from Late Antiquity and throughout the Middle Ages: ancient holy sites were destroyed or converted to Christian churches, indigenous pagan gods were demonized, and traditional religious practices were condemned as witchcraft and even criminalized -- sometimes upon penalty of death.
Martin of Tours	Martin of Tours was a Bishop of Tours whose shrine became a famous stopping-point for pilgrims on the road to Santiago de Compostela. Around his name much legendary material accrued, and he has become one of the most familiar and recognizable Christian saints. He is considered a spiritual bridge across Europe, given his association with both France and Hungary.
Canterbury	1°05′13″E? / ?51.275°N 1.087°E? / 51.275; 1.087 Canterbury is an English city which lies at the heart of the City of Canterbury, a district of Kent in South East England. It lies on the River Stour. Originally a Brythonic settlement, it was renamed Durovernum Cantiacorum by the Roman conquerors in the 1st century AD. After it became the chief Jutish settlement, it gained its English name Canterbury, itself derived from the Old English Cantwareburh ('Kent people's stronghold').
Synod of Whitby	The Synod of Whitby was a seventh century Northumbrian synod where King Oswiu of Northumbria ruled that his kingdom would calculate Easter and observe the monastic tonsure according to the customs of Rome, rather than the customs practised by Iona and its satellite institutions. The synod was summoned in 664 at Saint Hilda's double monastery of Streonshalh (Streanæshalch), later called Whitby Abbey.
Conversion to Christianity	Conversion to Christianity is the religious conversion of a previously non-Christian person to some form of Christianity. It has been called the foundational experience of Christian life.

Conversion to Christianity primarily involves belief (faith) in God, repentance of sin, acknowledgement of falling far short of God's glory and holiness and confession of Jesus Christ as the Son of God and the all-sufficient and only means by whom one's sin can be atoned for and therefore the only route to salvation (John 14:6).

Jurisprudence

Jurisprudence is the study and theory of law. Scholars of jurisprudence, or legal theorists (including legal philosophers and social theorists of law), hope to obtain a deeper understanding of the nature of law, of legal reasoning, legal systems and of legal institutions. Modern jurisprudence began in the 18th century and was focused on the first principles of the natural law, civil law, and the law of nations.

Bubonic plague

Bubonic plague is a zoonotic disease, circulating mainly among small rodents and their fleas, and is one of three types of infections caused by Yersinia pestis (formerly known as Pasteurella pestis), which belongs to the family Enterobacteriaceae. Without treatment, the bubonic plague kills about two out of three infected humans within 4 days.

The term bubonic plague is derived from the Greek word bubo, meaning 'swollen gland'.

Cyrillic alphabet

The Cyrillic alphabet is an alphabetic writing system developed in the First Bulgarian Empire during the 10th century AD at the Preslav Literary School. It is used in various languages, past and present, of Eastern Europe and Asia, especially those of Slavic origin, and also non-Slavic languages influenced by Russian.

The alphabet is derived from the Ancient Greek uncial script, augmented by ligatures and consonants from the older Glagolitic alphabet for sounds not found in Ancient Greek. It is named in honor of the two Byzantine Greek brothers, Saints Cyril and Methodius, who created the Glagolitic alphabet earlier on. Modern scholars consider that Cyrillic was developed and formalized by early disciples of Cyril and Methodius (such as Clement of Ohrid).

Orthodox Christianity

The term Orthodox Christianity may refer to•Eastern Orthodoxy: the Ancient communion of Eastern Christian Churches, historically of eastern Europe and parts of Asia, that recognize the Council of Chalcedon and the other of the first seven Ecumenical Councils.•Oriental Orthodoxy: the Miaphysite Eastern Christian churches adhering to the first three Ecumenical Councils and the 449 Council of Ephesus, and rejecting the Council of Chalcedon and the later councils that Eastern Orthodoxy classifies as ecumenical.

Secret History

Secret History was a long-running British television documentary series. Shown on Channel 4, the Secret History brandname was used as a banner title in the UK, but many of the individual documentaries can still be found on US cable channels (like Discovery Times or The History Channel International) without the branding. It can be seen as Channel 4's answer to the BBC's Timewatch.

7. Late Antiquity, 250-600

CHAPTER HIGHLIGHTS & NOTES: KEY TERMS, PEOPLE, PLACES, CONCEPTS

Third Rome	The term Third Rome describes the idea that some European city, state, or country is the successor to the legacy of ancient Rome (the 'first Rome') and, according to different perspectives, either via connection to the Byzantine Empire (also known as the 'Eastern Roman Empire') as being the 'second Rome'; or via connection to the Western Roman Empire via connection to its claimed successors such as the Papal States or the Holy Roman Empire as being the 'second Rome'. Russian claims Within decades after the capture of Constantinople by Mehmed II of the Ottoman Empire on 29 May 1453, some Eastern Orthodox people were nominating Moscow as the 'Third Rome', or the 'New Rome'. Stirrings of this sentiment began during the reign of Ivan III of Russia who had married Sophia Paleologue.

CHAPTER QUIZ: KEY TERMS, PEOPLE, PLACES, CONCEPTS

1. A _________ is a structured hymn used in a number of Eastern Orthodox services. It consists of nine odes, sometimes called canticles or songs depending on the translation, based on the Biblical canticles. Most of these are found in the Old Testament, but the final ode is taken from the Magnificat and Song of Zechariah from the New Testament.

   a. Canticle
   b. Carmelite Rite
   c. Canon
   d. Compline

2. The _________ was a seventh century Northumbrian synod where King Oswiu of Northumbria ruled that his kingdom would calculate Easter and observe the monastic tonsure according to the customs of Rome, rather than the customs practised by Iona and its satellite institutions. The synod was summoned in 664 at Saint Hilda's double monastery of Streonshalh (Streanæshalch), later called Whitby Abbey.

   a. Synod of Whitby
   b. Vergilius of Salzburg
   c. Christianization of Lithuania
   d. Praying town

3. . The _________ is an alphabetic writing system developed in the First Bulgarian Empire during the 10th century AD at the Preslav Literary School. It is used in various languages, past and present, of Eastern Europe and Asia, especially those of Slavic origin, and also non-Slavic languages influenced by Russian.

   The alphabet is derived from the Ancient Greek uncial script, augmented by ligatures and consonants from the older Glagolitic alphabet for sounds not found in Ancient Greek. It is named in honor of the two Byzantine Greek brothers, Saints Cyril and Methodius, who created the Glagolitic alphabet earlier on.

Modern scholars consider that Cyrillic was developed and formalized by early disciples of Cyril and Methodius (such as Clement of Ohrid).

a. Erik the Red
b. Philosophy of music
c. Neurophilosophy
d. Cyrillic alphabet

4. The _________ is the creed or profession of faith that is most widely used in Christian liturgy. It is called Nicene ( ) because, in its original form, it was adopted in the city of Nicaea by the first ecumenical council, which met there in the year 325.

The _________ has been normative for the Anglican Church, the Church of the East, the Eastern Orthodox Church, the Oriental Orthodox churches, the Roman Catholic Church including the Eastern Catholic Churches, the Old Catholic Church, the Lutheran Church and many Protestant denominations, forming the eponymous mainstream definition of Christianity itself in Nicene Christianity.

a. Palamism
b. Paul of Samosata
c. Nicene Creed
d. Semi-Arianism

5. The _________ is a term used by modern historians to distinguish the Constantinople-centred Roman Empire of the Middle Ages from its earlier classical existence. It is also referred to as the Eastern Roman Empire, primarily in the context of Late Antiquity, while the Empire was still administered with separate eastern and western political centres. Its citizens continued to refer to their empire as the Roman Empire or Romania .

a. Cardium Pottery
b. The Corrupting Sea A Study of Mediterranean History
c. Fatimid Caliphate
d. Byzantine Empire

Visit Cram101.com for full Practice Exams

ANSWER KEY
7. Late Antiquity, 250-600

1. c
2. a
3. d
4. c
5. d

You can take the complete Chapter Practice Test

for 7. Late Antiquity, 250-600
on all key terms, persons, places, and concepts.

Online 99 Cents

http://www.epub141.56.21995.7.cram101.com/

Use www.Cram101.com for all your study needs

including Cram101's online interactive problem solving labs in

chemistry, statistics, mathematics, and more.

8. Europe in the Early Middle Ages, 600-1000

CHAPTER OUTLINE: KEY TERMS, PEOPLE, PLACES, CONCEPTS

- Early Middle Ages
- Middle Ages
- Early Christianity
- Bedouin
- Society
- Jesus of Nazareth
- Prophet
- Byzantine Empire
- Last Judgment
- Abu Bakr
- Five Pillars of Islam
- Iberian Peninsula
- Arab world
- Merovingian dynasty
- Civitas
- Duke
- Alamanni
- Carolingian Empire
- Lombards
- Charlemagne
- Dalmatia

8. Europe in the Early Middle Ages, 600-1000

CHAPTER OUTLINE: KEY TERMS, PEOPLE, PLACES, CONCEPTS

Bishop

Fertile Crescent

Emigration

Carolingian Renaissance

Carolingian minuscule

Ebbo

Missal

Psalter

Christianity

Lindisfarne

Lindisfarne Gospels

Anglo-Saxons

Beowulf

Louis the German

Louis the Pious

Treaty of Verdun

Viking

Continental Europe

Danegeld

Danelaw

Macedonians

Visit Cram101.com for full Practice Exams

8. Europe in the Early Middle Ages, 600-1000

CHAPTER OUTLINE: KEY TERMS, PEOPLE, PLACES, CONCEPTS

_______________ Orthodox Christianity

_______________ Varangians

_______________ Battle of Lechfeld

_______________ Boyar

_______________ Feudalism

CHAPTER HIGHLIGHTS & NOTES: KEY TERMS, PEOPLE, PLACES, CONCEPTS

Early Middle Ages

The Early Middle Ages was the period of European history lasting from the 5th century to the 10th century. The Early Middle Ages followed the decline of the Western Roman Empire and preceded the High Middle Ages (c. 1001-1300). The period saw a continuation of trends begun during late classical antiquity, including population decline, especially in urban centres, a decline of trade, and increased immigration.

Middle Ages

The Middle Ages is a stretch of European history that lasted from the 5th until the 15th centuries. It began with the collapse of the Western Roman Empire, and was followed by the Renaissance and the Age of Discovery. The Middle Ages is the middle period of the traditional division of Western history into Classical, Medieval, and Modern periods.

Early Christianity

Early Christianity is generally considered as Christianity before 325. The New Testament's Book of Acts and Epistle to the Galatians records that the first Christian community was centered in Jerusalem and its leaders included James, Peter and John.

The first Christians were all Jews or Jewish proselytes, either by birth or conversion, referred to by historians as the Jewish Christians. Paul of Tarsus, after his conversion, claimed the title of 'Apostle to the Gentiles'.

Bedouin

The Bedouin (from the Arabic badawi , pl. badw) are a part of the predominantly desert-dwelling Arab ethnic group. Specifically the term refers only to the 'Camel-raising' tribes, but due to economic changes many are now settled or raising sheep.

8. Europe in the Early Middle Ages, 600-1000

Society

A society, is a group of people related to each other through persistent relations, or a large social grouping sharing the same geographical or virtual territory, subject to the same political authority and dominant cultural expectations. Human societies are characterized by patterns of relationships (social relations) between individuals who share a distinctive culture and institutions; a given society may be described as the sum total of such relationships among its constituent members. In the social sciences, a larger society often evinces stratification and/or dominance patterns in subgroups.

Jesus of Nazareth

Jesus of Nazareth is the first volume in Pope Benedict XVI's planned three-volume meditation on the life and teachings of Jesus Christ. The first book authored by Benedict since his ascension to the papacy, it was published by Doubleday in 2007.

In the book's introduction, the pope explicitly states that the treatise is in 'no way an exercise of the magisterium,' but rather an 'expression of his personal search for the face of the Lord.'

Jesus of Nazareth's ten chapters cover the bulk of Jesus' public ministry, encompassing subjects and events such as Christ's baptism at the hands of John the Baptist, the Sermon on the Mount, the meaning of the parables, the Calling of the Twelve, the Confession of Peter, and the Transfiguration.

Prophet

In religion, a prophet is an individual who is claimed to have been contacted by the supernatural or the divine, and serves as an intermediary with humanity, delivering this newfound knowledge from the supernatural entity to other people. The message that the prophet conveys is called a prophecy.

Claims of prophets have existed in many cultures through history, including Judaism, Christianity, Islam, the Sybilline and the Pythia, known as the Oracle of Delphi, in Ancient Greece, Zoroaster, the Völuspá in Old Norse and many others.

Byzantine Empire

The Byzantine Empire is a term used by modern historians to distinguish the Constantinople-centred Roman Empire of the Middle Ages from its earlier classical existence. It is also referred to as the Eastern Roman Empire, primarily in the context of Late Antiquity, while the Empire was still administered with separate eastern and western political centres. Its citizens continued to refer to their empire as the Roman Empire or Romania .

Last Judgment

The Last Judgment is a canonical fresco by the Italian Renaissance master Michelangelo executed on the altar wall of the Sistine Chapel in Vatican City. The work took four years to complete and was done between 1536 and 1541 (preparation of the altar wall began in 1535). Michelangelo began working on it some twenty years after having finished the Sistine Chapel ceiling.

Abu Bakr

Abu Bakr was a senior companion (Sahabah) and the father-in-law of the Islamic Prophet Muhammad.

Visit Cram101.com for full Practice Exams

He ruled over the Rashidun Caliphate from 632-634 CE when he became the first Muslim Caliph following Muhammad's death. As Caliph, Abu Bakr succeeded to the political and administrative functions previously exercised by the Prophet, since the religious function and authority of prophethood ended with Muhammad's death according to Islam.

Five Pillars of Islam

The Five Pillars of Islam are five basic acts in Islam, considered obligatory by Sunni Muslims. These are summarized in the famous Hadith of Gabriel.

The Qur'an presents them as a framework for worship and a sign of commitment to the faith. They are (1) the shahada (creed), (2) daily prayers (salat), (3) fasting during Ramadan (sawm), (4) almsgiving (zakat), and (5) the pilgrimage to Mecca (hajj) at least once in a lifetime.

Iberian Peninsula

The Iberian Peninsula, commonly called Iberia, is a peninsula located in the extreme southwest of Europe and includes the modern-day sovereign states of Spain, Portugal, Andorra and France, as well as the British Overseas Territory of Gibraltar. It is the westernmost of the three major southern European peninsulas-the Iberian, Italian, and Balkan peninsulas. It is bordered on the southeast and east by the Mediterranean Sea, and on the north, west and southwest by the Atlantic Ocean.

Arab world

The Arab world consists of the Arabic-speaking states and populations in North Africa, Western Asia and elsewhere.

The standard definition of the Arab world comprises the 22 states and territories of the Arab League stretching from the Atlantic Ocean in the west to the Arabian Sea in the east, and from the Mediterranean Sea in the north to the Horn of Africa and the Indian Ocean in the southeast. It has a combined population of around 340 million people, with over half under 25 years of age.

Merovingian dynasty

The Merovingians were a Salian Frankish dynasty that came to rule the Franks in a region known as Francia in Latin for 300 years from the middle of the 5th century, their territory largely corresponding to ancient Gaul as well as the Roman provinces of Raetia, Germania Superior and the southern part of Germania Magna. The Merovingian dynasty was founded by Childeric I (c.457 - 481) the son of Merovech, leader of the Salian Franks, but it was his famous son Clovis I (481 - 511) who united all of Gaul under Merovingian rule.

After the death of Clovis there were frequent clashes between different branches of the family, but when threatened by its neighbours the Merovingians presented a strong united front.

Civitas

In the history of Rome, the Latin term civitas, according to Cicero in the time of the late Roman Republic, was the social body of the cives, or citizens, united by law (concilium coetusque hominum jure sociati). It is the law that binds them together, giving them responsibilities (munera) on the one hand and rights of citizenship on the other.

8. Europe in the Early Middle Ages, 600-1000

CHAPTER HIGHLIGHTS & NOTES: KEY TERMS, PEOPLE, PLACES, CONCEPTS

Duke	A duke or duchess (female) can either be a monarch ruling over a duchy or a member of the nobility, historically of highest rank below the monarch. The title comes from French duc, itself from the Latin dux, 'leader', a term used in republican Rome to refer to a military commander without an official rank, and later coming to mean the leading military commander of a province. During the Middle Ages the title signified first among the Germanic monarchies.
Alamanni	The Alamanni, Allemanni, or Alemanni were originally an alliance of Germanic tribes located around the upper Rhine river . One of the earliest references to them is the cognomen Alamannicus assumed by Roman Emperor Caracalla, who ruled the Roman Empire from 211 to 217 and claimed thereby to be their conqueror. The nature of this alliance and their previous tribal affiliations remain uncertain.
Carolingian Empire	Carolingian Empire is a historiographical term referring to the realm of the Franks under the Carolingian dynasty in the Early Middle Ages. This dynasty is seen as the origin of modern France and Germany, with its beginning date based upon the crowning of Charlemagne, or Charles the Great, as western emperor, and its end with the death of Charles the Fat. Depending on one's perspective, the Carolingian Empire may be seen as the later history of the Frankish Realm or the early history of the Kingdom of France and of the Holy Roman Empire.
Lombards	The Lombards, were a Germanic tribe who ruled a Kingdom in Italy from 568 to 774. The Lombard historian Paul the Deacon wrote in the Historia Langobardorum that the Lombards descended from a small tribe called the Winnili who dwelt in southern Scandinavia (Scadanan) before migrating to seek new lands. In the 1st century AD they formed part of the Suebi, in northwestern Germany.
Charlemagne	Charlemagne was King of the Franks from 768 and Emperor of the Romans (Imperator Romanorum) from 800 to his death in 814. He expanded the Frankish kingdom into an empire that incorporated much of Western and Central Europe. During his reign, he conquered Italy and was crowned Imperator Augustus by Pope Leo III on 25 December 800. This temporarily made him a rival of the Byzantine Emperor in Constantinople. His rule is also associated with the Carolingian Renaissance, a revival of art, religion, and culture through the medium of the Catholic Church.
Dalmatia	The Theme of Dalmatia was a Byzantine theme (a military-civilian province) on the eastern coast of the Adriatic Sea in Southeastern Europe, headquartered at Zadar. Origins Dalmatia first came under Byzantine control in the 530s, when the generals of Emperor Justinian I (r. 527-565) seized it from the Ostrogoths in the Gothic War.

Bishop	In the Catholic Church, a bishop is an ordained minister who holds the fullness of the sacrament of Holy Orders and is responsible for teaching doctrine, governing Catholics in his jurisdiction, and sanctifying the world and for representing the Church. Catholics trace the origins of the office of bishop to the apostles, who were endowed with a special charism by the Holy Spirit at Pentecost. Catholics believe this special charism has been transmitted through an unbroken succession of bishops by the laying on of hands in the sacrament of Holy Orders.
Fertile Crescent	The Fertile Crescent is a region in Western Asia. It includes the comparatively fertile regions of Mesopotamia and the Levant, delimited by the dry climate of the Syrian Desert to the south and the Anatolian highlands to the north. The region is often considered the cradle of civilization; it saw the development of many of the earliest human civilizations, and is the birthplace of writing and the wheel.
Emigration	Emigration is the act of leaving one's country or region to settle in another. It is the same as immigration but from the perspective of the country of origin. Human movement before the establishment of political boundaries or within one state is termed migration.
Carolingian Renaissance	The Carolingian Renaissance was as a period of intellectual and cultural revival in the Carolingian Empire occurring from the late eighth century to the ninth century, as the first of three medieval renaissances. It occurred mostly during the reigns of the Carolingian rulers Charlemagne and Louis the Pious. It was supported by the scholars of the Carolingian court, notably Alcuin of York For moral betterment the Carolingian renaissance reached for models drawn from the example of the Christian Roman Empire of the 4th century.
Carolingian minuscule	Carolingian minuscule or Caroline minuscule is a script developed as a writing standard in Europe so that the Roman alphabet could be easily recognized by the literate class from one region to another. It was used in Charlemagne's empire between approximately 800 and 1200. Codices, pagan and Christian texts, and educational material were written in Carolingian minuscule throughout the Carolingian Renaissance. The script developed into blackletter and became obsolete, though its revival in the Italian renaissance forms the basis of more recent scripts.
Ebbo	Ebbo was archbishop of Rheims from 816 until 835 and again from 840 to 841. He was born a German serf on the royal demesne of Charlemagne. He was educated at his court and became the librarian and councillor of Louis the Pious, king of Aquitaine, son of Charlemagne. When Louis became emperor, he appointed Ebbo to the see of Rheims, then vacant after the death of Wulfaire.
Missal	A missal is a liturgical book containing all instructions and texts necessary for the celebration of Mass throughout the year. Before the compilation of such books, several books were used when celebrating Mass.

Psalter

A psalter is a volume containing the Book of Psalms, often with other devotional material bound in as well, such as a liturgical calendar and litany of the Saints. Until the later medieval emergence of the book of hours, psalters were the books most widely owned by wealthy lay persons and were commonly used for learning to read. Many Psalters were richly illuminated and they include some of the most spectacular surviving examples of medieval book art.

Christianity

Christianity is a monotheistic and Abrahamic religion based on the life and teachings of Jesus Christ as presented in canonical gospels and other New Testament writings. Most adherents of the Christian faith, known as Christians, believe that Jesus is the Son of God, fully divine and fully human and the savior of humanity prophesied in the Old Testament. Consequentially, Christians commonly refer to Jesus as Christ or Messiah.

Lindisfarne

1°47′44″W? / ?55.6713°N 1.7955°W? / 55.6713; -1.7955

Lindisfarne is a tidal island off the north-east coast of England also known as Holy Island, the name of the civil parish. Both the Parker Chronicle and Peterborough Chronicle annals of AD793 record the Old English name, Lindisfarena, which means 'island [of the] travellers from Lindsey', indicating that the island was settled from Lindsey, or possibly that its inhabitants travelled there. In 2001 the island had a population of 162.

Lindisfarne Gospels

The Lindisfarne Gospels is an illuminated manuscript gospel book produced around the year 700 AD in a monastery off the coast of Northumberland at Lindisfarne and which is now on display in the British Library in London. The manuscript is one of the finest works in the unique style of Hiberno-Saxon or Insular art, combining Mediterranean, Anglo-Saxon and Celtic elements.

The Lindisfarne Gospels are presumed to be the work of a monk named Eadfrith, who became Bishop of Lindisfarne in 698 and died in 721. Current scholarship indicates a date around 715, and it is believed they were produced in honour of St. Cuthbert.

Anglo-Saxons

The Anglo-Saxons were the population in Britain partly descended from the Germanic tribes who migrated from continental Europe and settled the south and east of the island beginning in the early 5th century. The Anglo-Saxon period denotes the period of English history after their initial settlement through their creation of the English nation, up to the Norman conquest; that is, between about 550 and 1066. The term Anglo-Saxon is also used for the language, today more correctly called Old English, that was spoken and written by the Anglo-Saxons in England (and parts of south-eastern Scotland) between at least the mid-5th century and the mid-12th century, after which it is known as Middle English.

The Benedictine monk Bede, writing in the early 8th century, identified the English as the descendants of three Germanic tribes:•the Angles, who probably came from Angeln : Bede wrote that their whole nation came to Britain, leaving their former land empty.

Beowulf

Etymology and origins of the character

A number of origins have been proposed for the name Beowulf. Bee-Wolf

Henry Sweet, a philologist and early linguist specializing in Germanic languages, proposed that the name Beowulf literally means in Old English 'bee-wolf' or 'bee-hunter' and that it is a kenning for 'bear'. This etymology is mirrored in recorded instances of similar names.

Louis the German

Louis (also Ludwig or Lewis) the German (806 - 28 August 876), also known as Louis II or Louis the Bavarian, was a grandson of Charlemagne and the third son of the succeeding Frankish Emperor Louis the Pious and his first wife, Ermengarde of Hesbaye.

He received the appellation 'Germanicus' shortly after his death in recognition of the fact that the bulk of his territory had been in the former Germania.

Louis II was made the King of Bavaria from 817 following the Emperor Charlemagne's practice of bestowing a local kingdom on a family member who then served as one of his lieutenants and the local governor. When his father, Louis I (called the pious), partitioned the empire toward the end of his reign in 843, he was made King of East Francia, a region that spanned the Elbe drainage basin from Jutland southeasterly through the Thuringerwald into modern Bavaria from the Treaty of Verdun in 843 until his death. Divisio imperii and filial rebellion

His early years were partly spent at the court of his grandfather, Charlemagne, whose special affection he is said to have won. When the emperor Louis divided his dominions between his sons in 817, Louis received Bavaria and the neighbouring lands but did not undertake the governing of such until 825, when he became involved in wars with the Wends and Sorbs on his eastern frontier. In 827, he married Emma of Altdorf, sister of his stepmother Judith of Bavaria, and daughter of Welf, whose possessions ranged from Alsace to Bavaria. Louis soon began to interfere in the quarrels arising from Judith's efforts to secure a kingdom for her own son Charles (later known as Charles the Bald) and the consequent struggles of his brothers with their father.

His involvement in the first civil war of his father's reign was limited, but in the second, his elder brothers, Lothair, then King of Italy, and Pepin, King of Aquitaine, induced him to invade Alamannia -- which their father had given to their half-brother Charles -- by promising to give him the land in the new partition they would make. In 832, he led an army of Slavs into Alamannia and completely subjugated it. Louis the Pious disinherited him, but to no effect; the emperor was captured by his own rebellious sons and deposed. Upon his swift reinstatement, however, the Emperor Louis made peace with his son Louis and restored Bavaria (never actually lost) to him (836).

In the third civil war (began 839) of his father's ruinous final decade, Louis was the instigator. A strip of his land having been given to the young Charles, Louis invaded Alamannia again.

His father was not so sluggish in responding to him this time, and soon the younger Louis was forced into the far southeastern corner of his realm, the March of Pannonia. Peace had been made by force of arms. Civil war, 840-843

When the elder Louis died in 840, and Lothair claimed the whole Empire, Louis allied with the half-brother, Charles the Bald, and defeated Lothair and their nephew Pepin II of Aquitaine, son of Pepin, at the Battle of Fontenay in June 841. In June 842, the three brothers met on an island in the Saône to negotiate a peace, and each appointed forty representatives to arrange the boundaries of their respective kingdoms. This developed into the Treaty of Verdun, concluded in August 843, by which Louis received the bulk of the lands lying east of the Rhine (Eastern Francia), together with a district around Speyer, Worms, and Mainz, on the left bank of the river. His territories included Bavaria (where he made Regensburg the centre of his government), Thuringia, Franconia, and Saxony. He may truly be called the founder of the German kingdom, though his attempts to maintain the unity of the Empire proved futile. Having in 842 crushed the Stellinga rising in Saxony, in 844 he compelled the Obotrites to own his authority and put their prince, Gozzmovil, to death. Thachulf, Duke of Thuringia, then undertook campaigns against the Bohemians, Moravians, and other tribes, but was not very successful in freeing his shores from the ravages of the Vikings. Conflict with Charles the Bald

In 852, he had sent his son Louis the Younger to Aquitaine, where the nobles had grown resentful of Charles the Bald's rule. The younger Louis did not set out until 854, but he returned the following year. In 853 and the following years, Louis made more than one attempt to secure the throne of Western Francia, which, according to the Annals of Fulda (Annales Fuldenses), the people of that country offered him in their disgust with the cruel misrule of Charles the Bald. Encouraged by his nephews Pepin II and Charles, King of Provence, Louis invaded in 858; Charles the Bald could not even raise an army to resist the invasion and fled to Burgundy; in that year, Louis issued a charter dated 'the first year of the reign in West Francia.' Treachery and desertion in his army, and the loyalty to Charles of the Aquitanian bishops, brought about the failure of the enterprise, which Louis renounced by a treaty signed at Coblenz on 7 June 860.

In 855, the emperor Lothair died, and Louis and Charles for a time seem to have cooperated in plans to divide Lothair's possessions among themselves -- the only impediments to this being Lothair's sons: Lothair II (who received Lotharingia), Louis II (who held the imperial title and the Iron Crown), and the aforementioned Charles. In 868, at Metz they agreed definitely to a partition of Lotharingia; but when Lothair II died in 869, Louis the German was lying seriously ill, and his armies were engaged with the Moravians.

Louis the Pious

Louis the Pious also called the Fair, and the Debonaire, was the King of Aquitaine from 781. He was also King of the Franks and co-Emperor (as Louis I) with his father, Charlemagne, from 813. As the only surviving adult son of Charlemagne and Hildegard, he became the sole ruler of the Franks after his father's death in 814, a position which he held until his death, save for the period 833-34, during which he was deposed.

During his reign in Aquitaine, Louis was charged with the defence of the Empire's southwestern frontier. He conquered Barcelona from the Muslims in 801 and asserted Frankish authority over Pamplona and the Basques south of the Pyrenees in 812. As emperor he included his adult sons, Lothair, Pepin, and Louis, in the government and sought to establish a suitable division of the realm among them.

Treaty of Verdun

The Treaty of Verdun was first of the treaties that divided the Carolingian Empire in the 9th century. Three surviving sons of Louis the Pious, the son and successor of Charlemagne, divided the Carolingian Empire into three kingdoms. It ended the three-year-long Carolingian Civil War.

Viking

Viking is the name of the son of Vífil and Eimyrja in Þorsteins saga Víkingssonar. Viking is the father of Thorsten and Thorer.

The two daughters of Logi (Haloge) were stolen away by suitors to nearby islands.

Continental Europe

Continental Europe, also referred to as mainland Europe or simply the Continent, is the continent of Europe, explicitly excluding European islands. Notably, in British English usage, the term means Europe excluding the United Kingdom, the Isle of Man, the Channel Islands, Ireland and Iceland.

One general definition of 'Continental Europe' is the European landmass excluding the UK, Ireland and Iceland.

Danegeld

The Danegeld was a tax raised to pay tribute to the Viking raiders to save a land from being ravaged. It was called the geld or gafol in eleventh-century sources; the term Danegeld did not appear until the early twelfth century. It was characteristic of royal policy in both England and Francia during the ninth through eleventh centuries, collected both as tributary, to buy off the attackers, and as stipendiary, to pay the defensive forces.

Danelaw

The Danelaw, as recorded in the Anglo-Saxon Chronicle, is a historical name given to the part of England in which the laws of the 'Danes' held sway and dominated those of the Anglo-Saxons. It is contrasted with 'West Saxon law' and 'Mercian law'. The term has been extended by modern historians to be geographical.

Macedonians

MacedoniansМакедонциMakedonci

The Macedonians (Macedonian: Македонци; transliterated: Makedonci) - also referred to as Macedonian Slavs - are a South Slavic people who are primarily associated with the Republic of Macedonia. They speak the Macedonian language, a South Slavic language. About two thirds of all ethnic Macedonians live in the Republic of Macedonia and there are also communities in a number of other countries.

Visit Cram101.com for full Practice Exams

8. Europe in the Early Middle Ages, 600-1000

CHAPTER HIGHLIGHTS & NOTES: KEY TERMS, PEOPLE, PLACES, CONCEPTS

Varangians

The Varangians, who between the 9th and the 11th centuries ruled the medieval state of Rus', and formed the Byzantine Varangian Guard.

According to the 12th century Kievan Primary Chronicle, a group of Varangians known as the Rus' settled in Novgorod in 6370 (862), under the leadership of Rurik. Before Rurik, the Rus' might have ruled an earlier hypothetical polity.

Battle of Lechfeld

The Battle of Lechfeld often seen as the defining event for holding off the incursions of the Hungarians into Western Europe, was a decisive victory by Otto I the Great, King of the Germans, over the Hungarian leaders, the harka (military leader) Bulcsú and the chieftains Lél (Lehel) and Súr. Located south of Augsburg, the Lechfeld is the flood plain that lies along the Lech River. The battle appears as the Battle of Augsburg in Hungarian historiography.

Boyar

A boyar, Kievan Rus'ian, Bulgarian, Wallachian, and Moldavian aristocracies, second only to the ruling princes (in Bulgaria, tsars), from the 10th century through the 17th century. The rank has lived on as a surname in Russia and Finland, where it is spelled 'Pajari'.

Etymology

According to most sources the word is of Proto-Bulgarian origin.

Feudalism

Feudalism was a set of legal and military customs in medieval Europe that flourished between the ninth and fifteenth centuries, which, broadly defined, was a system for ordering society around relationships derived from the holding of land in exchange for service or labour. Although derived from the Latin word feodum (fief), then in use, the term feudalism and the system it describes were not conceived of as a formal political system by the people living in the medieval period. In its classic definition, by François-Louis Ganshof (1944), feudalism describes a set of reciprocal legal and military obligations among the warrior nobility, revolving around the three key concepts of lords, vassals and fiefs.

1. In the history of Rome, the Latin term _________, according to Cicero in the time of the late Roman Republic, was the social body of the cives, or citizens, united by law (concilium coetusque hominum jure sociati). It is the law that binds them together, giving them responsibilities (munera) on the one hand and rights of citizenship on the other. The agreement (concilium) has a life of its own, creating a res publica or 'public entity' , into which individuals are born or accepted, and from which they die or are ejected.

   a. Tullus Hostilius
   b. Congius
   c. Civitas
   d. Deposition of Romulus Augustulus

2. The _________ are five basic acts in Islam, considered obligatory by Sunni Muslims. These are summarized in the famous Hadith of Gabriel.

   The Qur'an presents them as a framework for worship and a sign of commitment to the faith. They are (1) the shahada (creed), (2) daily prayers (salat), (3) fasting during Ramadan (sawm), (4) almsgiving (zakat), and (5) the pilgrimage to Mecca (hajj) at least once in a lifetime.

   a. Second Servile War
   b. Five Pillars of Islam
   c. Fatimid Caliphate
   d. Fertile Crescent

3. The _________ was the period of European history lasting from the 5th century to the 10th century. The _________ followed the decline of the Western Roman Empire and preceded the High Middle Ages (c. 1001-1300). The period saw a continuation of trends begun during late classical antiquity, including population decline, especially in urban centres, a decline of trade, and increased immigration.

   a. Second Servile War
   b. Baptism of Poland
   c. History of Christianity in Ukraine
   d. Early Middle Ages

4. . Etymology and origins of the character

   A number of origins have been proposed for the name _________. Bee-Wolf

   Henry Sweet, a philologist and early linguist specializing in Germanic languages, proposed that the name _________ literally means in Old English 'bee-wolf' or 'bee-hunter' and that it is a kenning for 'bear'. This etymology is mirrored in recorded instances of similar names.

   a. Cofgod
   b. Fetch

c. Beowulf
d. Harrow on the Hill

5. _________ or Caroline minuscule is a script developed as a writing standard in Europe so that the Roman alphabet could be easily recognized by the literate class from one region to another. It was used in Charlemagne's empire between approximately 800 and 1200. Codices, pagan and Christian texts, and educational material were written in _________ throughout the Carolingian Renaissance. The script developed into blackletter and became obsolete, though its revival in the Italian renaissance forms the basis of more recent scripts.

a. Erik the Red
b. Celtic brooch
c. Carolingian minuscule
d. Cloth of St Gereon

Visit Cram101.com for full Practice Exams

ANSWER KEY
8. Europe in the Early Middle Ages, 600-1000

1. c
2. b
3. d
4. c
5. c

You can take the complete Chapter Practice Test

for 8. Europe in the Early Middle Ages, 600-1000
on all key terms, persons, places, and concepts.

Online 99 Cents

http://www.epub141.56.21995.8.cram101.com/

Use www.Cram101.com for all your study needs

including Cram101's online interactive problem solving labs in

chemistry, statistics, mathematics, and more.

9. State and Church in the High Middle Ages, 1000-1300

CHAPTER OUTLINE: KEY TERMS, PEOPLE, PLACES, CONCEPTS

High Middle Ages

Middle Ages

Bayeux Tapestry

Anglo-Saxons

Domesday Book

Capetian dynasty

Gascony

Hugh Capet

Primogeniture

Battle of Lechfeld

Charlemagne

Duchy

French revolution

Hundred Years' War

Holy Roman Empire

Iberian Peninsula

Kingdom of the Two Sicilies

Kingdom of Sicily

Granada

Duke

Magna Carta

9. State and Church in the High Middle Ages, 1000-1300

CHAPTER OUTLINE: KEY TERMS, PEOPLE, PLACES, CONCEPTS

______ Margrave

______ Christianity

______ Gregorian Reform

______ Christian Church

______ College of Cardinals

______ Periculoso

______ Canon law

______ Lateran Council

______ Canon

______ Church

______ Sacrament

______ Religious violence

______ First Crusade

______ Crusader states

______ Saladin

______ Seventh Crusade

______ Third Crusade

______ Fourth Crusade

______ Teutonic Knights

______ Deicide

______ Baltic region

Visit Cram101.com for full Practice Exams

9. State and Church in the High Middle Ages, 1000-1300

CHAPTER OUTLINE: KEY TERMS, PEOPLE, PLACES, CONCEPTS

_______________ Albert the Bear

_______________ Eastern Europe

_______________ Christendom

CHAPTER HIGHLIGHTS & NOTES: KEY TERMS, PEOPLE, PLACES, CONCEPTS

High Middle Ages

The High Middle Ages was the period of European history around the 11th, 12th, and 13th centuries (c. 1000-1300). The High Middle Ages were preceded by the Early Middle Ages and followed by the Late Middle Ages, which by convention end around 1500.

The key historical trend of the High Middle Ages was the rapidly increasing population of Europe, which brought about great social and political change from the preceding era.

Middle Ages

The Middle Ages is a stretch of European history that lasted from the 5th until the 15th centuries. It began with the collapse of the Western Roman Empire, and was followed by the Renaissance and the Age of Discovery. The Middle Ages is the middle period of the traditional division of Western history into Classical, Medieval, and Modern periods.

Bayeux Tapestry

The Bayeux Tapestry is an embroidered cloth-not an actual tapestry-nearly 70 metres (230 ft) long, which depicts the events leading up to the Norman conquest of England concerning William, Duke of Normandy and Harold, Earl of Wessex, later King of England, and culminating in the Battle of Hastings.

According to Sylvette Lemagnen, conservator of the tapestry,'

The Bayeux tapestry is one of the supreme achievements of the Norman Romanesque, ... Its survival almost intact over nine centuries is little short of miraculous, ... Its exceptional length, the harmony and freshness of its colors, its exquisite workmanship, and the genius of its guiding spirit combine to make it endlessly fascinating. '

The tapestry consists of some fifty scenes with Latin tituli (captions), embroidered on linen with coloured woollen yarns.

9. State and Church in the High Middle Ages, 1000-1300

CHAPTER HIGHLIGHTS & NOTES: KEY TERMS, PEOPLE, PLACES, CONCEPTS

Anglo-Saxons

The Anglo-Saxons were the population in Britain partly descended from the Germanic tribes who migrated from continental Europe and settled the south and east of the island beginning in the early 5th century. The Anglo-Saxon period denotes the period of English history after their initial settlement through their creation of the English nation, up to the Norman conquest; that is, between about 550 and 1066. The term Anglo-Saxon is also used for the language, today more correctly called Old English, that was spoken and written by the Anglo-Saxons in England (and parts of south-eastern Scotland) between at least the mid-5th century and the mid-12th century, after which it is known as Middle English.

The Benedictine monk Bede, writing in the early 8th century, identified the English as the descendants of three Germanic tribes:•the Angles, who probably came from Angeln : Bede wrote that their whole nation came to Britain, leaving their former land empty.

Domesday Book

Domesday Book, now held at The National Archives, Kew,in South West London, is the record of the great survey of much of England and parts of Wales completed in 1086. The survey was executed for William I of England (William the Conqueror): 'While spending the Christmas time of 1085 in Gloucester, William had deep speech with his counsellors and sent men all over England to each shire to find out what or how much each landholder had in land and livestock, and what it was worth' (Anglo-Saxon Chronicle).

One of the main purposes of the survey was to determine who held what and what taxes had been liable under Edward the Confessor; the judgment of the Domesday assessors was final--whatever the book said about who held the material wealth or what it was worth, was the law, and there was no appeal. It was written in Latin, although there were some vernacular words inserted for native terms with no previous Latin equivalent, and the text was highly abbreviated.

Capetian dynasty

The Capetian dynasty, is among the largest and oldest European royal houses, consisting of the descendants of King Hugh Capet of France in the male line. In contemporary times, both King Juan Carlos of Spain and Grand Duke Henri of Luxembourg are members of this family, both through the Bourbon branch of the dynasty. Name origins and usage

The name of the dynasty derives from its founder, Hugh, who was known as 'Hugh Capet'.

Gascony

Gascony is an area of southwest France that was part of the 'Province of Guyenne and Gascony' prior to the French Revolution. The region is vaguely defined and the distinction between Guyenne and Gascony is unclear; sometimes they are considered to overlap, and sometimes Gascony is considered a part of Guyenne. Most definitions put Gascony east and south of Bordeaux.

Hugh Capet

Hugh Capet, called in contemporary sources 'Hugh the Great', was the first 'King of the Franks' of the eponymous Capetian dynasty from his election to succeed the Carolingian Louis V in 987 until his death. Descent and inheritance

The son of Hugh the Great, Duke of France, and Hedwige of Saxony, daughter of the German king Henry the Fowler, Hugh was born in 941. His paternal family, the Robertians, were powerful landowners in the Île-de-France. His grandfather had been King Robert I. His grandmother Beatrice was a Carolingian, a daughter of Herbert I of Vermandois.

Primogeniture

Primogeniture is the right, by law or custom, of the firstborn to inherit the entire estate, to the exclusion of younger siblings (compare to ultimogeniture). Historically, the term implied male primogeniture, to the exclusion of females. According to the Norman tradition, the first-born son inherited the entirety of a parent's wealth, estate, title or office and then would be responsible for any further passing of the inheritance to his siblings.

Battle of Lechfeld

The Battle of Lechfeld often seen as the defining event for holding off the incursions of the Hungarians into Western Europe, was a decisive victory by Otto I the Great, King of the Germans, over the Hungarian leaders, the harka (military leader) Bulcsú and the chieftains Lél (Lehel) and Súr. Located south of Augsburg, the Lechfeld is the flood plain that lies along the Lech River. The battle appears as the Battle of Augsburg in Hungarian historiography.

Charlemagne

Charlemagne was King of the Franks from 768 and Emperor of the Romans (Imperator Romanorum) from 800 to his death in 814. He expanded the Frankish kingdom into an empire that incorporated much of Western and Central Europe. During his reign, he conquered Italy and was crowned Imperator Augustus by Pope Leo III on 25 December 800. This temporarily made him a rival of the Byzantine Emperor in Constantinople. His rule is also associated with the Carolingian Renaissance, a revival of art, religion, and culture through the medium of the Catholic Church.

Duchy

Grand Duchies •Grand Duchy of Baden•Grand Duchy of Finland•Grand Duchy of Hesse•Grand Duchy of Lithuania•Grand Duchy of Luxembourg•Grand Duchy of TuscanyDuchies in Austria, Germany, Italy, and the Low Countries •Duchy of Acerenza•Duchy of Alsace•Duchy of Apulia•Duchy of Austria•Duchy of Bavaria•Duchy of Brabant•Duchy of Bremen•Duchy of Brunswick•Duchy of Carinthia•Duchy of Carniola•Duchy of Ferrara•Duchy of Franconia•Duchy of Gelders•Duchy of Holstein•Duchy of Lauenburg•Duchy of Limburg•Duchy of Upper Lorraine•Duchy of Lower Lorraine•Duchy of Luxemburg•Duchy of Magdeburg•Duchy of Mantua•Duchy of Mecklenburg•Duchy of Milan•Duchy of Modena•Duchy of Oldenburg•Duchy of Parma•Duchy of Pomerania•Duchy of Salzburg•Duchy of Savoy•Duchy of Saxony•Duchy of Schleswig•Duchy of Spoleto•Duchy of Styria•Duchy of Swabia•Duchy of WürttembergDuchy in Denmark •Duchy of SchleswigDuchies in England •Duchy of Cornwall•Duchy of LancasterDuchies in France •Duchy of Anjou•Duchy of Aquitaine•Duchy of Berry•Duchy of Bourbon•Duchy of Brittany•Duchy of Burgundy•Duchy of Normandy•Duchy of OrléansDuchies in Poland •Duchy of Prussia•Duchy of WarsawOther current or historical duchies •United Baltic Duchy•Littoral Croatian Duchy•Duchy of the Franks•Duchy of Gascony•Duchy of Limburg•Duchy of Rascia•Duchy of Vasconia•Duchy of Athens.

9. State and Church in the High Middle Ages, 1000-1300

CHAPTER HIGHLIGHTS & NOTES: KEY TERMS, PEOPLE, PLACES, CONCEPTS

French revolution

The French Revolution, was a period of radical social and political upheaval in France that had a lasting impact on French history and more broadly throughout the world. The absolute monarchy that had ruled France for centuries collapsed within three years. French society underwent an epic transformation, as feudal, aristocratic and religious privileges evaporated under a sustained assault from radical left-wing political groups, masses on the streets, and peasants in the countryside.

Hundred Years' War

The Hundred Years' War was a series of wars waged from 1337 to 1453 by the House of Valois and the House of Plantagenet, also known as the House of Anjou, for the French throne, which had become vacant upon the extinction of the senior Capetian line of French kings. The House of Valois claimed the title of King of France, while the Plantagenets claimed the thrones of both France and England. The Plantagenet kings were the 12th-century rulers of the kingdom of England, and had their roots in the French regions of Anjou and Normandy.

Holy Roman Empire

The Holy Roman Empire was a varying complex of lands that existed from 962 to 1806 in Central Europe. It grew out of East Francia, one of the primary divisions of the Frankish Empire. Its character changed during the Middle Ages and the Early Modern period, when the power of the emperor gradually weakened in favour of the princes.

Iberian Peninsula

The Iberian Peninsula, commonly called Iberia, is a peninsula located in the extreme southwest of Europe and includes the modern-day sovereign states of Spain, Portugal, Andorra and France, as well as the British Overseas Territory of Gibraltar. It is the westernmost of the three major southern European peninsulas-the Iberian, Italian, and Balkan peninsulas. It is bordered on the southeast and east by the Mediterranean Sea, and on the north, west and southwest by the Atlantic Ocean.

Kingdom of the Two Sicilies

The Kingdom of the Two Sicilies was the largest of the Italian states before Italian unification. It was formed of a union of the Spanish Bourbon Kingdom of Sicily and the Kingdom of Naples, which collectively had long been called the 'Two Sicilies' (Utriusque Siciliae), in 1816 and lasted until 1860, when it was annexed by the Kingdom of Sardinia, which became the Kingdom of Italy in 1861. The Two Sicilies had its capital in Naples and was commonly referred to in English as the 'Kingdom of Naples'. The kingdom extended over the Mezzogiorno (the southern part of mainland Italy) and the island of Sicily.

Kingdom of Sicily

The Kingdom of Sicily was a state that existed in the south of Italy from its founding by Roger II in 1130 until 1816. It was a successor state of the County of Sicily, which had been founded in 1071 during the Norman conquest of southern Italy. Until 1282 the Kingdom (sometimes called the regnum Apuliae et Siciliae) covered not only the island of Sicily, but also the whole Mezzogiorno region of southern Italy and the Maltese archipelago. The island was divided into three regions: Val di Mazara, Val Demone and Val di Noto.

Granada

Granada is a 2009 German-style board game developed by Dirk Henn and published by Queen Games. It is based on and heavily inspired by Henn's earlier game, the Spiel des Jahres-winning Alhambra.

Duke

A duke or duchess (female) can either be a monarch ruling over a duchy or a member of the nobility, historically of highest rank below the monarch. The title comes from French duc, itself from the Latin dux, 'leader', a term used in republican Rome to refer to a military commander without an official rank, and later coming to mean the leading military commander of a province.

During the Middle Ages the title signified first among the Germanic monarchies.

Magna Carta

Magna Carta, is an Angevin charter originally issued in Latin in the year 1215. It was translated into vernacular French as early as 1219, and reissued later in the 13th century in modified versions. The later versions excluded the most direct challenges to the monarch's authority that had been present in the 1215 charter. The charter first passed into law in 1225; the 1297 version, with the long title 'The Great Charter of the Liberties of England, and of the Liberties of the Forest,' still remains on the statute books of England and Wales.

Margrave

A margrave was a medieval hereditary nobleman with military responsibilities in a border province of a kingdom. Border provinces usually had more exposure to military incursions from the outside, compared to interior provinces, and thus a margrave usually had larger and more active military forces than other lords. The margrave may also have had larger territorial area under his control as a result of expansions of territory at the border.

Christianity

Christianity is a monotheistic and Abrahamic religion based on the life and teachings of Jesus Christ as presented in canonical gospels and other New Testament writings. Most adherents of the Christian faith, known as Christians, believe that Jesus is the Son of God, fully divine and fully human and the savior of humanity prophesied in the Old Testament. Consequentially, Christians commonly refer to Jesus as Christ or Messiah.

Gregorian Reform

The Gregorian Reforms were a series of reforms initiated by Pope Gregory VII and the circle he formed in the papal curia, circa 1050-80, which dealt with the moral integrity and independence of the clergy. These reforms are considered to be named after Pope Gregory VII (1073-85), though he personally denied this and claimed his reforms, like his regnal name, honored Gregory the Great.

Although at each new turn the reforms were presented to contemporaries as a return to the old ways, they are often seen by modern historians as the first European Revolution.

Christian Church

The Christian Church is the assembly or association of followers of Jesus Christ. The Greek term ? κκλησ?α, which in its appearances in the New Testament is usually translated as 'church', basically means 'assembly'.

9. State and Church in the High Middle Ages, 1000-1300

CHAPTER HIGHLIGHTS & NOTES: KEY TERMS, PEOPLE, PLACES, CONCEPTS

College of Cardinals

The College of Cardinals is the body of all cardinals of the Catholic Church.

A function of the college is to advise the pope about church matters when he summons them to an ordinary consistory. It also convenes on the death or abdication of a pope as a papal conclave to elect a successor.

Periculoso

Periculoso was a papal decretal of Pope Boniface VIII issued in 1298, that required the claustration of Catholic nuns. It is often incorrectly referred to as a papal bull.

Canonical status

Periculoso was later incorporated into the Liber Sextus, a compilation of papal legislation.

Canon law

The canon law of the Catholic Church is a fully developed legal system, with all the necessary elements: courts, lawyers, judges, a fully articulated legal code and principles of legal interpretation. It lacks the necessary binding force present in most modern day legal systems. The academic degrees in canon law are the J.C.B. (Juris Canonici Baccalaureatus, Bachelor of Canon Law, normally taken as a graduate degree), J.C.L. (Juris Canonici Licentiatus, Licentiate of Canon Law) and the J.C.D. (Juris Canonici Doctor, Doctor of Canon Law).

Lateran Council

The Lateran Council of 769 was a synod held in the Basilica of St. John Lateran to rectify abuses in the papal electoral process which had led to the elevation of the Antipopes Constantine II and Philip It also condemned the rulings of the Council of Hieria. It is perhaps the most important Roman council held during the eight century.

The death of Pope Paul I saw the uncanonical election of two antipopes.

Canon

A canon is a structured hymn used in a number of Eastern Orthodox services. It consists of nine odes, sometimes called canticles or songs depending on the translation, based on the Biblical canticles. Most of these are found in the Old Testament, but the final ode is taken from the Magnificat and Song of Zechariah from the New Testament.

Church

In the Christian religion, a church is a building or structure to facilitate the meeting of its members. Originally, Jewish Christians met in synagogues, such as the Cenacle, and in one another's homes, known as house churches. As Christianity grew and became more accepted by governments, notably with the Edict of Milan, rooms and, eventually, entire buildings were set aside for the explicit purpose of Christian worship, such as the Church of the Holy Sepulcher.

Sacrament

In The Church of Jesus Christ of Latter-day Saints (LDS Church, commonly called Mormons), the Holy Sacrament of the Lord's Supper, most often simply referred to as the sacrament, is the sacrament in which participants partake of bread and drink water in remembrance of the body and blood of Jesus Christ.

It is similar in some ways, but different in others to the Eucharist in the Catholic Church, or communion or the Lord's Supper in other Christian denominations. Normally in LDS congregations, the sacrament is provided every Sunday as part of the sacrament meeting.

Religious violence

Religious violence is a term that covers phenomena where religion, in its diversity, is either the subject or object of violent behaviour. Religious violence is, specifically, violence that is motivated by or in reaction to religious precepts, texts, or doctrines. This includes violence against religious institutions, persons, objects, or when the violence is motivated to some degree by some religious aspect of the target or precept of the attacker.

First Crusade

The First Crusade was a military expedition by Roman Catholic Europe to regain the Holy Lands taken in the Muslim conquests of the Levant (632-661), ultimately resulting in the recapture of Jerusalem in 1099. It was launched on 27 November 1095 by Pope Urban II with the primary goal of responding to an appeal from Byzantine Emperor Alexios I Komnenos, who requested that western volunteers come to his aid and help to repel the invading Seljuq Turks from Anatolia. An additional goal soon became the principal objective--the Christian reconquest of the sacred city of Jerusalem and the Holy Land and the freeing of the Eastern Christians from Islamic rule.

During the crusade, knights and peasants from many nations of Western Europe travelled over land and by sea, first to Constantinople and then on towards Jerusalem, as crusaders; the peasants greatly outnumbered the knights.

Crusader states

The Crusader states were a number of mostly 12th- and 13th-century feudal states created by Western European crusaders in Asia Minor, Greece and the Holy Land (ancient and modern Israel and the Palestinian region). The name also refers to other territorial gains (often small and short-lived) made by medieval Christendom against Muslim and pagan adversaries.

Mediterranean

While the Reconquista, the centuries-long fight to reconquer the Iberian peninsula from the Arabized Berbers known as Moors (who called it al-Andalus), fills all the criteria for crusades, it is not customary to call the resulting Catholic principalities there Crusader states, except for the Kingdom of Valencia.

Saladin

?ala? ad-Din Yusuf ibn Ayyubi (c. 1138 - March 4, 1193), better known in the Western world as Saladin, was a Kurdish Muslim, who became the first Ayyubid Sultan of Egypt and Syria. He led Islamic opposition to the Franks and other European Crusaders in the Levant. At the height of his power, he ruled over Egypt, Syria, Mesopotamia, Hejaz, and Yemen.

Seventh Crusade

The Seventh Crusade was a crusade led by Louis IX of France from 1248 to 1254.

Approximately 800,000 bezants were paid in ransom for King Louis who, along with thousands of his troops, was captured and defeated by the Egyptian army led by the Ayyubid Sultan Turanshah supported by the Bahariyya Mamluks led by Faris ad-Din Aktai, Baibars al-Bunduqdari, Qutuz, Aybak and Qalawun.

In 1244, the Khwarezmians, recently displaced by the advance of the Mongols, took Jerusalem on their way to ally with the Egyptian Mamluks. This returned Jerusalem to Muslim control, but the fall of Jerusalem was no longer an earth-shattering event to European Christians, who had seen the city pass from Christian to Muslim control numerous times in the past two centuries.

Third Crusade

The Third Crusade also known as the Kings' Crusade, was an attempt by European leaders to reconquer the Holy Land from Saladin . It was largely successful, but fell short of its ultimate goal- the reconquest of Jerusalem.

After the failure of the Second Crusade, the Zengid dynasty controlled a unified Syria and engaged in a conflict with the Fatimid rulers of Egypt, which ultimately resulted in the unification of Egyptian and Syrian forces under the command of Saladin, who employed them to reduce the Christian states and to recapture Jerusalem in 1187. Spurred by religious zeal, Henry II of England and Philip II of France ended their conflict with each other to lead a new crusade.

Fourth Crusade

The Fourth Crusade was originally intended to conquer Muslim-controlled Jerusalem by means of an invasion through Egypt. Instead, in April 1204, the Crusaders of Western Europe invaded and sacked the Christian (Eastern Orthodox) city of Constantinople, capital of the Eastern Roman Empire (Byzantine Empire). This is seen as one of the final acts in the Great Schism between the Eastern Orthodox Church and Roman Catholic Church, and a key turning point in the decline of the Empire and of Christianity in the Near East.

Teutonic Knights

The Order of Brothers of the German House of Saint Mary in Jerusalem, commonly the Teutonic Order, is a German medieval military order, and in modern times a purely religious Catholic order. It was formed to aid Christians on their pilgrimages to the Holy Land and to establish hospitals. Its members have commonly been known as the Teutonic Knights, since they also served as a crusading military order in the Middle Ages.

Deicide

Deicide is the killing of a god. The term deicide was coined in the 17th century from medieval Latin *deicidium, from de-us 'god' and cidium 'cutting, killing.'

The concept is applied to the Crucifixion of Jesus specifically, but may be used to any act of killing a god, including a life-death-rebirth deity who is killed and then resurrected.

In Christianity, the concept was notably used in the question of guilt associated with a responsibility for the death of Jesus.

Visit Cram101.com for full Practice Exams

Baltic region

The terms Baltic region, Baltic Rim countries, and Baltic Rim refer to slightly different combinations of countries in the general area surrounding the Baltic Sea.

Etymology

The first to name it the Baltic Sea ('Mare Balticum') was eleventh century German chronicler Adam of Bremen.

Denotation

Depending on the context the Baltic region might stand for:•The countries that have shorelines along the Baltic Sea: Denmark, Estonia, Latvia, Finland, Germany, Lithuania, Poland, Russia, and Sweden.•The group of countries presently referred to by the short-hand Baltic states: Estonia, Latvia, and Lithuania, sometimes in addition the Russian Kaliningrad exclave.•Historic East Prussia and the historical lands of Livonia, Courland and Estonia .•The former Baltic province of Imperial Russia: Today's Estonia, Latvia, Lithuania .•The countries on the historical British trade route through the Baltic Sea, i.e. including the Scandinavian Peninsula (Sweden and Norway).•The Council of the Baltic Sea States, comprised by the countries with shorelines along the Baltic Sea, in addition to Norway, Iceland and the rest of European Union.•The islands of the Euroregion B7 Baltic Seven Islands, which includes the islands and archipelagos Åland (autonomous), Bornholm (Denmark), Gotland (Sweden), Hiiumaa (Estonia), Öland (Sweden), Rügen, and Saaremaa (Estonia).•On historic Scandinavian and German maps, the Balticum sometimes includes only the historically or culturally German-dominated lands, or provinces, of Estonia, Livonia, Courland and Latgale (corresponding to modern Estonia and Latvia), as well as sometimes Pommerania and East Prussia, while the historically less-Germanized Lithuania is occasionally excluded..

Albert the Bear

Albert the Bear was the first Margrave of Brandenburg (as Albert I) from 1157 to his death and was briefly Duke of Saxony between 1138 and 1142.

Albert was the only son of Otto, Count of Ballenstedt, and Eilika, daughter of Magnus Billung, Duke of Saxony. He inherited the valuable estates in northern Saxony of his father in 1123, and on his mother's death, in 1142, succeeded to one-half of the lands of the house of Billung.

Eastern Europe

Eastern Europe is the eastern part of the European continent. The term has widely disparate and varying geopolitical, geographical, cultural and socioeconomic readings, which makes it highly context-dependent and even volatile, and there are 'almost as many definitions of Eastern Europe as there are scholars of the region'. A related United Nations paper adds that 'every assessment of spatial identities is essentially a social and cultural construct'.

Christendom

Christendom, has several meanings. In a cultural sense, it refers to the worldwide community of Christians, adherents of Christianity.

9. State and Church in the High Middle Ages, 1000-1300

CHAPTER QUIZ: KEY TERMS, PEOPLE, PLACES, CONCEPTS

1. The _________, was a period of radical social and political upheaval in France that had a lasting impact on French history and more broadly throughout the world. The absolute monarchy that had ruled France for centuries collapsed within three years. French society underwent an epic transformation, as feudal, aristocratic and religious privileges evaporated under a sustained assault from radical left-wing political groups, masses on the streets, and peasants in the countryside.

   a. Erik the Red
   b. French revolution
   c. Federal monarchy
   d. Gatekeeper state

2. _________ is an area of southwest France that was part of the 'Province of Guyenne and _________' prior to the French Revolution. The region is vaguely defined and the distinction between Guyenne and _________ is unclear; sometimes they are considered to overlap, and sometimes _________ is considered a part of Guyenne. Most definitions put _________ east and south of Bordeaux.

   a. Second Servile War
   b. Fairhair dynasty
   c. Gausian dynasty
   d. Gascony

3. The _________ is an embroidered cloth-not an actual tapestry-nearly 70 metres (230 ft) long, which depicts the events leading up to the Norman conquest of England concerning William, Duke of Normandy and Harold, Earl of Wessex, later King of England, and culminating in the Battle of Hastings.

   According to Sylvette Lemagnen, conservator of the tapestry,'

   The _________ is one of the supreme achievements of the Norman Romanesque, ... Its survival almost intact over nine centuries is little short of miraculous, ... Its exceptional length, the harmony and freshness of its colors, its exquisite workmanship, and the genius of its guiding spirit combine to make it endlessly fascinating. '

   The tapestry consists of some fifty scenes with Latin tituli (captions), embroidered on linen with coloured woollen yarns.

   a. Bayeux Tapestry
   b. Benedictional of St. thelwold
   c. Rev. William Slater Calverley
   d. Canterbury-St Martin's hoard

4. .

   The _________ was the period of European history around the 11th, 12th, and 13th centuries (c. 1000-1300). The _________ were preceded by the Early Middle Ages and followed by the Late Middle Ages, which by convention end around 1500.

The key historical trend of the _________ was the rapidly increasing population of Europe, which brought about great social and political change from the preceding era.

a. Gascon Rolls
b. Peter Helias
c. High Middle Ages
d. Gualdim Pais

5. The _________ was originally intended to conquer Muslim-controlled Jerusalem by means of an invasion through Egypt. Instead, in April 1204, the Crusaders of Western Europe invaded and sacked the Christian (Eastern Orthodox) city of Constantinople, capital of the Eastern Roman Empire (Byzantine Empire). This is seen as one of the final acts in the Great Schism between the Eastern Orthodox Church and Roman Catholic Church, and a key turning point in the decline of the Empire and of Christianity in the Near East.

a. Fourth Crusade
b. Navarrese Company
c. Nicaean-Latin Armistice of 1260
d. Treaty of Nymphaeum

ANSWER KEY

9. State and Church in the High Middle Ages, 1000-1300

1. b

2. d

3. a

4. c

5. a

You can take the complete Chapter Practice Test

for 9. State and Church in the High Middle Ages, 1000-1300
on all key terms, persons, places, and concepts.

Online 99 Cents

http://www.epub141.56.21995.9.cram101.com/

Use www.Cram101.com for all your study needs

including Cram101's online interactive problem solving labs in

chemistry, statistics, mathematics, and more.

10. The Life of the People in the High Middle Ages, 1000-1300

CHAPTER OUTLINE: KEY TERMS, PEOPLE, PLACES, CONCEPTS

- High Middle Ages
- Middle Ages
- Apothecary
- Last Judgment
- Primogeniture
- Hagiography
- Veneration
- Christianity
- Eucharist
- Sacrament
- Passover
- Purgatory
- Chivalry
- Tournament
- Cistercians
- Bernard of Clairvaux
- Second Crusade
- Choir monk
- Hildegard of Bingen

High Middle Ages

The High Middle Ages was the period of European history around the 11th, 12th, and 13th centuries (c. 1000-1300). The High Middle Ages were preceded by the Early Middle Ages and followed by the Late Middle Ages, which by convention end around 1500.

The key historical trend of the High Middle Ages was the rapidly increasing population of Europe, which brought about great social and political change from the preceding era.

Middle Ages

The Middle Ages is a stretch of European history that lasted from the 5th until the 15th centuries. It began with the collapse of the Western Roman Empire, and was followed by the Renaissance and the Age of Discovery. The Middle Ages is the middle period of the traditional division of Western history into Classical, Medieval, and Modern periods.

Apothecary

Apothecary is a historical name for a medical professional who formulates and dispenses materia medica to physicians, surgeons and patients -- a role now served by a pharmacist (or a chemist or dispensing chemist) and some caregivers.

In addition to pharmacy responsibilities, the apothecary offered general medical advice and a range of services that are now performed solely by other specialist practitioners, such as surgery and midwifery. Apothecaries often operated through a retail shop which, in addition to ingredients for medicines, sold tobacco and patent medicines.

Last Judgment

The Last Judgment is a canonical fresco by the Italian Renaissance master Michelangelo executed on the altar wall of the Sistine Chapel in Vatican City. The work took four years to complete and was done between 1536 and 1541 (preparation of the altar wall began in 1535). Michelangelo began working on it some twenty years after having finished the Sistine Chapel ceiling.

Primogeniture

Primogeniture is the right, by law or custom, of the firstborn to inherit the entire estate, to the exclusion of younger siblings (compare to ultimogeniture). Historically, the term implied male primogeniture, to the exclusion of females. According to the Norman tradition, the first-born son inherited the entirety of a parent's wealth, estate, title or office and then would be responsible for any further passing of the inheritance to his siblings.

Hagiography

Hagiography is the study of saints. A hagiography, from the Greek (h)agios and graphe , refers literally to writings on the subject of such holy people, and specifically to the biographies of ecclesiastical and secular leaders. The term hagiology, the study of hagiography, is also current in English, though less common.

Veneration

Veneration, is the act of honoring a saint, a person who has been identified as having a high degree of sanctity or holiness. Angels are shown similar veneration in many religions.

10. The Life of the People in the High Middle Ages, 1000-1300

CHAPTER HIGHLIGHTS & NOTES: KEY TERMS, PEOPLE, PLACES, CONCEPTS

Christianity

Christianity is a monotheistic and Abrahamic religion based on the life and teachings of Jesus Christ as presented in canonical gospels and other New Testament writings. Most adherents of the Christian faith, known as Christians, believe that Jesus is the Son of God, fully divine and fully human and the savior of humanity prophesied in the Old Testament. Consequentially, Christians commonly refer to Jesus as Christ or Messiah.

Eucharist

The Eucharist, Sacrament of the Altar, the Blessed Sacrament, or The Lord's Supper, and other names, is a Christian sacrament or ordinance, generally considered to be a re-enactment of the Last Supper, the final meal that Jesus Christ shared with his disciples before his arrest and crucifixion, during which he gave them bread, saying, 'This is my body', and wine, saying, 'This is my blood'.

There are different interpretations of the significance of the Eucharist, but 'there is more of a consensus among Christians about the meaning of the Eucharist than would appear from the confessional debates over the sacramental presence, the effects of the Eucharist, and the proper auspices under which it may be celebrated.'

The phrase 'the Eucharist' may refer not only to the rite but also to the consecrated bread (leavened or unleavened) and wine or, unfermented grape juice (in some Protestant denominations) or water (in Mormonism), used in the rite, and, in this sense, communicants may speak of 'receiving the Eucharist', as well as 'celebrating the Eucharist'.

Names and their origin

Eucharist, from Greek ε?χαριστ?α (eucharistia), means 'thanksgiving'.

Sacrament

In The Church of Jesus Christ of Latter-day Saints (LDS Church, commonly called Mormons), the Holy Sacrament of the Lord's Supper, most often simply referred to as the sacrament, is the sacrament in which participants partake of bread and drink water in remembrance of the body and blood of Jesus Christ. It is similar in some ways, but different in others to the Eucharist in the Catholic Church, or communion or the Lord's Supper in other Christian denominations. Normally in LDS congregations, the sacrament is provided every Sunday as part of the sacrament meeting.

Passover

Christian Passover is a religious observance celebrated by some churches to keep faith with Old Testament teaching. It is often linked to the Christian holiday and festival of Easter. Often, only an abbreviated seder is celebrated to explain the meaning in a time-limited ceremony.

Purgatory

Purgatory is the condition or process of purification or temporary punishment in which, it is believed, the souls of those who die in a state of grace are made ready for Heaven. This is an idea that has ancient roots and is well-attested in early Christian literature, while the conception of purgatory as a geographically situated place is largely the creation of medieval Christian piety and imagination.

Visit Cram101.com for full Practice Exams

Chivalry

Chivalry is a term related to the medieval (Middle Ages) institution of knighthood which has an aristocratic military origin of individual training and service to others. It is usually associated with ideals of knightly virtues, honor and courtly love: 'the source of the chivalrous idea,' remarked Johan Huizinga, who devoted several chapters of The Waning of the Middle Ages to chivalry and its effects on the medieval character, 'is pride aspiring to beauty, and formalized pride gives rise to a conception of honour, which is the pole of noble life.'

Etymology

In English, the word is first attested in 1292, as a loan from Old French chevalerie 'knighthood', an abstract noun formed in the 11th century based on chevalier 'knight', ultimately from Medieval Latin caballarius 'horseman'; cavalry is from the Italian form of the same word, loaned via Middle French into English around 1540.

Between the 11th century and 15th centuries medieval writers often used the word chivalry, in meanings that changed over time, generally moving from the concrete meaning of 'status or fee associated with military follower owning a war horse' towards the moral ideal of the Christian warrior ethos propagated in the Romance genre which became popular in the 12th century, and the ideal of courtly love propagated in the contemporary Minnesang and related genres.

Tournament

A tournament, or tourney is the name popularly given to chivalrous competitions or mock fights of the Middle Ages and Renaissance (12th to 16th centuries). It is one of various types of hastiludes.

Of the several medieval definitions of the tournament given by Du Cange (Glossarium, s.v. 'Tourneamentum'), the best is that of Roger of Hoveden, who described tournaments as 'military exercises carried out, not in the knight's spirit of hostility(nullo interveniente odio), but solely for practice and the display of prowess (pro solo exercitio, atque ostentatione virium).'Origins

Equestrian games of war are known from before the Romans: for example, chariot racing and the like were popular in Celtic Europe.

Cistercians

The Order of Cistercians is a Catholic religious order of enclosed monks and nuns. They are sometimes also called the Bernardines or the White Monks, in reference to the colour of the habit, over which a black scapular is worn. The emphasis of Cistercian life is on manual labour and self-sufficiency, and many abbeys have traditionally supported themselves through activities such as agriculture and brewing ales. It was in this village that a group of Benedictine monks from the monastery of Molesme founded Cîteaux Abbey in 1098, with the goal of following more closely the Rule of Saint Benedict.

Bernard of Clairvaux

Bernard of Clairvaux, O.Cist (1090 - August 20, 1153) was a French abbot and the primary builder of the reforming Cistercian order.

After the death of his mother, Bernard sought admission into the Cistercian order. Three years later, he was sent to found a new abbey at an isolated clearing in a glen known as the Val d'Absinthe, about 15 km southeast of Bar-sur-Aube.

Second Crusade — The Second Crusade was the second major crusade launched from Europe. The Second Crusade was started in response to the fall of the County of Edessa the previous year to the forces of Zengi. The county had been founded during the First Crusade (1096-1099) by Baldwin of Boulogne in 1098. While it was the first Crusader state to be founded, it was also the first to fall.

Choir monk — In Roman Catholicism the term 'Choir Monk' is used to distinguish monks who may become priests from the lay brothers who are occupied mainly with secular affairs.

Hildegard of Bingen — Saint Hildegard of Bingen, O.S.B. (1098 - 17 September 1179), also known as Saint Hildegard, and Sibyl of the Rhine, was a German writer, composer, philosopher, Christian mystic, Benedictine abbess, visionary, and polymath. Elected a magistra by her fellow nuns in 1136, she founded the monasteries of Rupertsberg in 1150 and Eibingen in 1165. One of her works as a composer, the Ordo Virtutum, is an early example of liturgical drama and arguably the oldest surviving morality play.

She wrote theological, botanical and medicinal texts, as well as letters, liturgical songs, and poems, while supervising brilliant miniature Illuminations.

CHAPTER QUIZ: KEY TERMS, PEOPLE, PLACES, CONCEPTS

1. _________ is a historical name for a medical professional who formulates and dispenses materia medica to physicians, surgeons and patients -- a role now served by a pharmacist (or a chemist or dispensing chemist) and some caregivers.

   In addition to pharmacy responsibilities, the _________ offered general medical advice and a range of services that are now performed solely by other specialist practitioners, such as surgery and midwifery. _________(ies) often operated through a retail shop which, in addition to ingredients for medicines, sold tobacco and patent medicines.

   a. Edward the Martyr
   b. Apothecary
   c. Horses in the Middle Ages
   d. Lupus Protospatharius

2. .

The _________ was the period of European history around the 11th, 12th, and 13th centuries (c. 1000-1300). The _________ were preceded by the Early Middle Ages and followed by the Late Middle Ages, which by convention end around 1500.

The key historical trend of the _________ was the rapidly increasing population of Europe, which brought about great social and political change from the preceding era.

a. High Middle Ages
b. Peter Helias
c. Leges inter Brettos et Scottos
d. Gualdim Pais

3. In Roman Catholicism the term '_________' is used to distinguish monks who may become priests from the lay brothers who are occupied mainly with secular affairs.

a. Choir monk
b. Collegium Canisianum
c. Collegium Russicum
d. Colwyn Bay Deanery

4. _________ is a term related to the medieval (Middle Ages) institution of knighthood which has an aristocratic military origin of individual training and service to others. It is usually associated with ideals of knightly virtues, honor and courtly love: 'the source of the chivalrous idea,' remarked Johan Huizinga, who devoted several chapters of The Waning of the Middle Ages to _________ and its effects on the medieval character, 'is pride aspiring to beauty, and formalized pride gives rise to a conception of honour, which is the pole of noble life.'

Etymology

In English, the word is first attested in 1292, as a loan from Old French chevalerie 'knighthood', an abstract noun formed in the 11th century based on chevalier 'knight', ultimately from Medieval Latin caballarius 'horseman'; cavalry is from the Italian form of the same word, loaned via Middle French into English around 1540.

Between the 11th century and 15th centuries medieval writers often used the word _________, in meanings that changed over time, generally moving from the concrete meaning of 'status or fee associated with military follower owning a war horse' towards the moral ideal of the Christian warrior ethos propagated in the Romance genre which became popular in the 12th century, and the ideal of courtly love propagated in the contemporary Minnesang and related genres.

a. Courtly love
b. Chivalry
c. Julia Antonia
d. Soul cake

5. The _________, Sacrament of the Altar, the Blessed Sacrament, or The Lord's Supper, and other names, is a Christian sacrament or ordinance, generally considered to be a re-enactment of the Last Supper, the final meal that Jesus Christ shared with his disciples before his arrest and crucifixion, during which he gave them bread, saying, 'This is my body', and wine, saying, 'This is my blood'.

   There are different interpretations of the significance of the _________, but 'there is more of a consensus among Christians about the meaning of the _________ than would appear from the confessional debates over the sacramental presence, the effects of the _________, and the proper auspices under which it may be celebrated.'

   The phrase 'the _________' may refer not only to the rite but also to the consecrated bread (leavened or unleavened) and wine or, unfermented grape juice (in some Protestant denominations) or water (in Mormonism), used in the rite, and, in this sense, communicants may speak of 'receiving the _________', as well as 'celebrating the _________'.

   Names and their origin

   _________, from Greek ε?χαριστ?α (eucharistia), means 'thanksgiving'.

   a. Eucharist
   b. Advent
   c. Intertestamental period
   d. Incident at Antioch

Visit Cram101.com for full Practice Exams

ANSWER KEY
10. The Life of the People in the High Middle Ages, 1000-1300

1. b
2. a
3. a
4. b
5. a

You can take the complete Chapter Practice Test

for 10. The Life of the People in the High Middle Ages, 1000-1300
on all key terms, persons, places, and concepts.

Online 99 Cents

http://www.epub141.56.21995.10.cram101.com/

Use www.Cram101.com for all your study needs

including Cram101's online interactive problem solving labs in

chemistry, statistics, mathematics, and more.

11. The Creativity and Challenges of Medieval Cities, 1100-1300

CHAPTER OUTLINE: KEY TERMS, PEOPLE, PLACES, CONCEPTS

Middle Ages

Bruges

Brussels

Tournai

Apothecary

Communion

Hanseatic League

Correspondence

Avignon Papacy

Commercial Revolution

Jurisprudence

Justinian

Canon law

Constantine the African

Gratian

Henry de Bracton

Roman law

Siete Partidas

Astrolabe

Thomas Aquinas

High Middle Ages

11. The Creativity and Challenges of Medieval Cities, 1100-1300

CHAPTER OUTLINE: KEY TERMS, PEOPLE, PLACES, CONCEPTS

	Troubadour
	Romanesque architecture
	Medieval architecture
	Gregorian Reform
	Peter Waldo
	Waldensians
	Cistercians
	Clare of Assisi
	Franciscan
	Inquisition
	Friar

CHAPTER HIGHLIGHTS & NOTES: KEY TERMS, PEOPLE, PLACES, CONCEPTS

Middle Ages

The Middle Ages is a stretch of European history that lasted from the 5th until the 15th centuries. It began with the collapse of the Western Roman Empire, and was followed by the Renaissance and the Age of Discovery. The Middle Ages is the middle period of the traditional division of Western history into Classical, Medieval, and Modern periods.

Bruges

Bruges is the capital and largest city of the province of West Flanders in the Flemish Region of Belgium. It is located in the northwest of the country.

The historic city centre is a prominent World Heritage Site of UNESCO. It is oval-shaped and about 430 hectares in size.

Brussels

Brussels, officially the Brussels Region or Brussels-Capital Region, is the de facto capital of Belgium and of the European Union (EU).

It is also the largest urban area in Belgium, comprising 19 municipalities, including the municipality of the City of Brussels, which is the de jure capital of Belgium, in addition to the seat of the French Community of Belgium and of the Flemish Community.

Brussels has grown from a 10th-century fortress town founded by a descendant of Charlemagne into a metropolis of more than one million inhabitants.

Tournai

Tournai is a Walloon city and municipality of Belgium located 85 kilometres southwest of Brussels, on the river Scheldt, in the province of Hainaut.

Along with Tongeren, Tournai is the oldest city in Belgium and it has played an important role in the country's cultural history.

Geography

Tournai is located in the lowlands of Belgium, at the southern limit of the Flemish plain, in the basin of the river Scheldt .

Apothecary

Apothecary is a historical name for a medical professional who formulates and dispenses materia medica to physicians, surgeons and patients -- a role now served by a pharmacist (or a chemist or dispensing chemist) and some caregivers.

In addition to pharmacy responsibilities, the apothecary offered general medical advice and a range of services that are now performed solely by other specialist practitioners, such as surgery and midwifery. Apothecaries often operated through a retail shop which, in addition to ingredients for medicines, sold tobacco and patent medicines.

Communion

The Communion is the Gregorian chant sung during the distribution of the Eucharist in the Roman Rite Catholic Mass. It is one of the antiphonal chants of the Proper of the Mass, and the final chant in the proper. It is followed by the Post-Communion.

Hanseatic League

The Hanseatic League was an economic alliance of trading cities and their merchant guilds that dominated trade along the coast of Northern Europe. It stretched from the Baltic to the North Sea and inland during the Late Middle Ages and early modern period (c. 13th-17th centuries).

The League was created to protect commercial interests and privileges granted by foreign rulers in cities and countries the merchants visited.

Correspondence

In theology, correspondence is the relationship between spiritual and natural realities, or between mental and physical realities.

Pierre A.

Riffard : 'The doctrine of analogy and correspondence, present in all esoteric schools of thinking, upholds that the Whole is One and that its different levels (realms, worlds) are equivalent systems, whose parts are in strict correspondence. So much so that a part in a realm symbolically reflects and interacts with the corresponding part in another realm.

Avignon Papacy

The Avignon Papacy was the period from 1309 to 1376, during which seven successive popes resided in Avignon, in modern-day France, rather than in Rome. This situation arose from the conflict between the Papacy and the French crown.

Following the strife between Boniface VIII and Philip IV of France, and the death of his successor Benedict XI after only eight months in office, a deadlocked conclave finally elected Clement V, a Frenchman, as Pope in 1305. Clement declined to move to Rome, remaining in France, and in 1309 moved his court to the papal enclave at Avignon, where it remained for the next 67 years.

Commercial Revolution

The Commercial Revolution was a period of European economic expansion, colonialism, and mercantilism which lasted from approximately the 16th century until the early 18th century. It was succeeded in the mid-18th century by the Industrial Revolution. Beginning with the Crusades, Europeans rediscovered spices, silks, and other commodities rare in Europe.

Jurisprudence

Jurisprudence is the study and theory of law. Scholars of jurisprudence, or legal theorists (including legal philosophers and social theorists of law), hope to obtain a deeper understanding of the nature of law, of legal reasoning, legal systems and of legal institutions. Modern jurisprudence began in the 18th century and was focused on the first principles of the natural law, civil law, and the law of nations.

Justinian

Justinian (ISBN 0-8125-4527-3), was published in 1998 by Tor Books. It is a novel by American writer Harry Turtledove writing under the pseudonym H. N. Turteltaub, a name he uses when writing historical fiction.

Turtledove later used the Turteltaub name when writing a series of books about traders in post-Alexandrian Greece.

Canon law

The canon law of the Catholic Church is a fully developed legal system, with all the necessary elements: courts, lawyers, judges, a fully articulated legal code and principles of legal interpretation. It lacks the necessary binding force present in most modern day legal systems. The academic degrees in canon law are the J.C.B. (Juris Canonici Baccalaureatus, Bachelor of Canon Law, normally taken as a graduate degree), J.C.L. (Juris Canonici Licentiatus, Licentiate of Canon Law) and the J.C.D. (Juris Canonici Doctor, Doctor of Canon Law).

Constantine the African

Constantine the African was a Tunisian doctor of the eleventh century. The first part of his life was spent in Tunisia and the rest in Italy.

Gratian

Gratian, was a 12th century canon lawyer from Bologna. He is sometimes incorrectly referred to as Franciscus Gratianus, Johannes Gratianus, or Giovanni Graziano. The dates of his birth and death are unknown.

Henry de Bracton

Henry de Bracton (ca. 1210-68) was an English jurist. He is famous now for his writings on Law, particularly De Legibus et Consuetudinibus Angliae (On the Laws and Customs of England), and his ideas on mens rea, or criminal intent. According to Bracton, it was only through the examination of a combination of action and intention that the commission of a criminal act could be established. He also wrote on kingship, arguing that a ruler should only be called 'king', if he obtained and exercised power in a lawful manner.

Roman law

Roman law is the legal system of ancient Rome, and the legal developments which occurred before the seventh century AD -- when the Roman-Byzantine state adopted Greek as the language of government. The development of Roman law comprises more than a thousand years of jurisprudence -- from the Twelve Tables (ca. 439 BC) to the Corpus Juris Civilis (AD 528-35) ordered by Emperor Justinian I. This Roman law, the Justinian Code, was effective in the Eastern Roman (Byzantine) Empire (331-1453), and also served as a basis for legal practice in continental Europe, as well as in Ethiopia, and most former colonies of European nations, including Latin America.

Historically, 'Roman law' also denotes the legal system applied in most of Western Europe, until the end of the 18th century. In Germany, Roman law practice remained longer, having been the Holy Roman Empire (963-1816); thus the great influence upon the civil law systems in Europe.

Siete Partidas

The Siete Partidas was a Castilian statutory code first compiled during the reign of Alfonso X of Castile (1252-1284), with the intent of establishing a uniform body of normative rules for the kingdom. The codified and compiled text was originally called the Libro de las Leyes (Book of Laws). It was not until the 14th century that it was given its present name, referring to the number of sections into which it is divided.

Astrolabe

An astrolabe is a historical astronomical instrument used by astronomers, navigators, and astrologers. Its many uses include locating and predicting the positions of the Sun, Moon, planets, and stars; determining local time given local latitude and vice-versa; surveying; triangulation; and to cast horoscopes. They were used in Classical Antiquity and through the Islamic Golden Age and the European Middle Ages and Renaissance for all these purposes.

Thomas Aquinas

Thomas Aquinas, O.P. , also Thomas of Aquin or Aquino, was an Italian Dominican priest of the Roman Catholic Church, and an immensely influential philosopher and theologian in the tradition of scholasticism, known as Doctor Angelicus ([the] Angelic Doctor), Doctor Communis, or Doctor Universalis. 'Aquinas' is not a surname, but is a Latin demonym for a resident of Aquino, his place of birth. He was the foremost classical proponent of natural theology, and the father of Thomism.

11. The Creativity and Challenges of Medieval Cities, 1100-1300

CHAPTER HIGHLIGHTS & NOTES: KEY TERMS, PEOPLE, PLACES, CONCEPTS

High Middle Ages

The High Middle Ages was the period of European history around the 11th, 12th, and 13th centuries (c. 1000-1300). The High Middle Ages were preceded by the Early Middle Ages and followed by the Late Middle Ages, which by convention end around 1500.

The key historical trend of the High Middle Ages was the rapidly increasing population of Europe, which brought about great social and political change from the preceding era.

Troubadour

A troubadour was a composer and performer of Old Occitan lyric poetry during the High Middle Ages (1100-1350). Since the word 'troubadour' is etymologically masculine, a female troubadour is usually called a trobairitz.

The troubadour school or tradition began in the 11th century in Occitania, but it subsequently spread into Italy, Spain, and even Greece.

Romanesque architecture

Romanesque architecture is an architectural style of Medieval Europe characterized by semi-circular arches. There is no consensus for the beginning date of the Romanesque architecture, with proposals ranging from the 6th to the 10th century. It developed in the 12th century into the Gothic style, characterised by pointed arches.

Medieval architecture

Medieval architecture is a term used to represent various forms of architecture common in Medieval Europe. Although it does represent a type of look that represents it. The main reason why it is called medival.

Gregorian Reform

The Gregorian Reforms were a series of reforms initiated by Pope Gregory VII and the circle he formed in the papal curia, circa 1050-80, which dealt with the moral integrity and independence of the clergy. These reforms are considered to be named after Pope Gregory VII (1073-85), though he personally denied this and claimed his reforms, like his regnal name, honored Gregory the Great.

Although at each new turn the reforms were presented to contemporaries as a return to the old ways, they are often seen by modern historians as the first European Revolution.

Peter Waldo

Peter Waldo, Valdo, Valdes, or Waldes (c. 1140 - c. 1218), also Pierre Vaudès or de Vaux, is credited as the founder of the Waldensians, a Christian spiritual movement of the Middle Ages, descendants of which still exist in various regions of southern Europe. Due to lack of reliable documentation there is a great degree of debate over Waldo's role in the Waldensian sect which may have existed before his leadership, while the French historian Thuanus dated his death to the year 1179.

Waldensians

Waldensians, Waldenses, Vallenses or Vaudois are names for a Christian movement which started in Lyon, France, in the late 1170s.

The movement was started partly in response to the schisms that had consumed the Catholic church in the 12th century and advocated a return to the vows of poverty and preaching of the Gospel as advocated by Jesus and his disciples in the New Testament. Originally a reform movement within the Catholic Church, the movement was declared heretical by 1215 and became persecuted by Church officials.

Cistercians

The Order of Cistercians is a Catholic religious order of enclosed monks and nuns. They are sometimes also called the Bernardines or the White Monks, in reference to the colour of the habit, over which a black scapular is worn. The emphasis of Cistercian life is on manual labour and self-sufficiency, and many abbeys have traditionally supported themselves through activities such as agriculture and brewing ales. It was in this village that a group of Benedictine monks from the monastery of Molesme founded Cîteaux Abbey in 1098, with the goal of following more closely the Rule of Saint Benedict.

Clare of Assisi

Clare of Assisi. (July 16, 1194 - August 11, 1253), born Chiara Offreduccio, is an Italian saint and one of the first followers of Saint Francis of Assisi. She founded the Order of Poor Ladies, a monastic religious order for women in the Franciscan tradition, and wrote their Rule of Life--the first monastic rule known to have been written by a woman.

Franciscan

Most Franciscans are members of Roman Catholic religious orders founded by Saint Francis of Assisi. Besides Roman Catholic communities, there are also Old Catholic, Anglican, and ecumenical Franciscan communities.

The most prominent group is the Order of Friars Minor, commonly called simply the 'Franciscans.' They seek to follow most directly the manner of life that Saint Francis led.

Inquisition

The Inquisition was a group of institutions within the judicial system of the Roman Catholic Church whose aim was to 'fight against heretics'. It started in 12th-century France to combat the spread of heresy and error, and was later expanded to other European countries, as well as throughout the Spanish and Portuguese empires in the Americas, Asia and Africa.

Historical phases of the Inquisition include: the Medieval Inquisition; the Spanish Inquisition; the Portuguese Inquisition; and the Roman Inquisition.

The term Inquisition can apply to any one of several institutions which fought against heretics within the justice system of the Roman Catholic Church.

Friar

A friar is a member of one of the mendicant orders.

Visit Cram101.com for full Practice Exams

11. The Creativity and Challenges of Medieval Cities, 1100-1300

CHAPTER HIGHLIGHTS & NOTES: KEY TERMS, PEOPLE, PLACES, CONCEPTS

Friars and monks

Friars differ from monks in that they are called to live the evangelical counsels (vows of poverty, chastity and obedience) in service to a community, rather than through cloistered asceticism and devotion. Whereas monks live cloistered away from the world in a self-sufficient community, friars are supported by donations or other charitable support.

CHAPTER QUIZ: KEY TERMS, PEOPLE, PLACES, CONCEPTS

1. In theology, _________ is the relationship between spiritual and natural realities, or between mental and physical realities. _________ and esotericism

   Pierre A. Riffard : 'The doctrine of analogy and _________, present in all esoteric schools of thinking, upholds that the Whole is One and that its different levels (realms, worlds) are equivalent systems, whose parts are in strict _________. So much so that a part in a realm symbolically reflects and interacts with the corresponding part in another realm.

   a. Cosmological argument
   b. Cosmotheology
   c. Correspondence
   d. Court of Conscience

2. The _________ is a stretch of European history that lasted from the 5th until the 15th centuries. It began with the collapse of the Western Roman Empire, and was followed by the Renaissance and the Age of Discovery. The _________ is the middle period of the traditional division of Western history into Classical, Medieval, and Modern periods.

   a. Geography of Scotland in the Middle Ages
   b. Horse transports in the Middle Ages
   c. Middle Ages
   d. Lupus Protospatharius

3. . _________ is a historical name for a medical professional who formulates and dispenses materia medica to physicians, surgeons and patients -- a role now served by a pharmacist (or a chemist or dispensing chemist) and some caregivers.

   In addition to pharmacy responsibilities, the _________ offered general medical advice and a range of services that are now performed solely by other specialist practitioners, such as surgery and midwifery. _________(ies) often operated through a retail shop which, in addition to ingredients for medicines, sold tobacco and patent medicines.

   a. Edward the Martyr

b. Apothecary
c. Charleroi
d. Bruges

4. _________ is the capital and largest city of the province of West Flanders in the Flemish Region of Belgium. It is located in the northwest of the country.

The historic city centre is a prominent World Heritage Site of UNESCO. It is oval-shaped and about 430 hectares in size.

a. Charleroi
b. Dendermonde
c. Bruges
d. Tielt

5. _________ is an architectural style of Medieval Europe characterized by semi-circular arches. There is no consensus for the beginning date of the _________, with proposals ranging from the 6th to the 10th century. It developed in the 12th century into the Gothic style, characterised by pointed arches.

a. Romanesque architecture
b. Saint Barbara Altarpiece
c. Schntgen Museum
d. Speech scroll

Visit Cram101.com for full Practice Exams

ANSWER KEY

11. The Creativity and Challenges of Medieval Cities, 1100-1300

1. c
2. c
3. b
4. c
5. a

You can take the complete Chapter Practice Test

for 11. The Creativity and Challenges of Medieval Cities, 1100-1300

on all key terms, persons, places, and concepts.

Online 99 Cents

http://www.epub141.56.21995.11.cram101.com/

Use www.Cram101.com for all your study needs

including Cram101's online interactive problem solving labs in

chemistry, statistics, mathematics, and more.

12. The Crisis of the Late Middle Ages, 1300-1450

CHAPTER OUTLINE: KEY TERMS, PEOPLE, PLACES, CONCEPTS

- Little Ice Age
- Climate change
- Bubonic plague
- Pandemic
- John VI Kantakouzenos
- Flagellant
- Tournai
- Capetian dynasty
- Hundred Years' War
- Salic law
- Longbow
- Duke
- Joan of Arc
- House of Commons
- Representative assembly
- Avignon Papacy
- Babylonian captivity
- Catholic Church
- Criticism
- Council of Constance
- Hussite

Visit Cram101.com for full Practice Exams

CHAPTER OUTLINE: KEY TERMS, PEOPLE, PLACES, CONCEPTS

_______________ University of Oxford

_______________ Antipope

_______________ Bridget of Sweden

_______________ Jacquerie

_______________ John Ball

_______________ Society

_______________ Middle Ages

_______________ Divine Comedy

CHAPTER HIGHLIGHTS & NOTES: KEY TERMS, PEOPLE, PLACES, CONCEPTS

Little Ice Age

The Little Ice Age was a period of cooling that occurred after the Medieval Warm Period (Medieval Climate Optimum). While it was not a true ice age, the term was introduced into the scientific literature by François E. Matthes in 1939. It has been conventionally defined as a period extending from the 16th to the 19th centuries, or alternatively, from about 1350 to about 1850, though climatologists and historians working with local records no longer expect to agree on either the start or end dates of this period, which varied according to local conditions. NASA defines the term as a cold period between AD 1550 and AD 1850 and notes three particularly cold intervals: one beginning about 1650, another about 1770, and the last in 1850, each separated by intervals of slight warming.

Climate change

Climate change is a significant and lasting change in the statistical distribution of weather patterns over periods ranging from decades to millions of years. It may be a change in average weather conditions or the distribution of events around that average (e.g., more or fewer extreme weather events). Climate change may be limited to a specific region or may occur across the whole Earth.

Bubonic plague

Bubonic plague is a zoonotic disease, circulating mainly among small rodents and their fleas, and is one of three types of infections caused by Yersinia pestis (formerly known as Pasteurella pestis), which belongs to the family Enterobacteriaceae. Without treatment, the bubonic plague kills about two out of three infected humans within 4 days.

12. The Crisis of the Late Middle Ages, 1300-1450

Pandemic

A pandemic is an epidemic of infectious disease that is spreading through human populations across a large region; for instance multiple continents, or even worldwide. A widespread endemic disease that is stable in terms of how many people are getting sick from it is not a pandemic. Further, flu pandemics generally exclude recurrences of seasonal flu.

John VI Kantakouzenos

John VI Kantakouzenos or Cantacuzenus was the Byzantine emperor from 1347 to 1354.

Born in Constantinople, John Kantakouzenos was the son of Michael Kantakouzenos, governor of the Morea. Through his mother Theodora Palaiologina Angelina, he was a descendant of the reigning house of Palaiologos.

Flagellant

Flagellants are practitioners of an extreme form of mortification of their own flesh by whipping it with various instruments.

Flagellantism was a 13th and 14th centuries movement, consisting of radicals in the Catholic Church. It began as a militant pilgrimage and was later condemned by the Catholic Church as heretical.

Tournai

Tournai is a Walloon city and municipality of Belgium located 85 kilometres southwest of Brussels, on the river Scheldt, in the province of Hainaut.

Along with Tongeren, Tournai is the oldest city in Belgium and it has played an important role in the country's cultural history.

Geography

Tournai is located in the lowlands of Belgium, at the southern limit of the Flemish plain, in the basin of the river Scheldt .

Capetian dynasty

The Capetian dynasty, is among the largest and oldest European royal houses, consisting of the descendants of King Hugh Capet of France in the male line. In contemporary times, both King Juan Carlos of Spain and Grand Duke Henri of Luxembourg are members of this family, both through the Bourbon branch of the dynasty. Name origins and usage

The name of the dynasty derives from its founder, Hugh, who was known as 'Hugh Capet'

Hundred Years' War

The Hundred Years' War was a series of wars waged from 1337 to 1453 by the House of Valois and the House of Plantagenet, also known as the House of Anjou, for the French throne, which had become vacant upon the extinction of the senior Capetian line of French kings. The House of Valois claimed the title of King of France, while the Plantagenets claimed the thrones of both France and England.

Salic law	Salic law, or Salian Law, was the major body of Frankish law governing all the Franks of Frankia under the rule of its kings during the Old Frankish Period, approximately equal to the early Middle Ages. The laws were maintained in written form in the Latin language by a committee empowered by the monarch. Dozens of manuscripts dated from the 8th century of a putative original recension in the 6th century and three emendations as late as the 9th century have survived.
Longbow	A longbow is a type of bow that is tall (roughly equal to the height of the person who uses it); this will allow its user a fairly long draw, at least to the jaw (the average length of arrowshafts recovered from the 1545 sinking of the Mary Rose is 75 cm/30 in). A longbow is not significantly recurved. Its limbs are relatively narrow so that they are circular or D-shaped in cross section.
Duke	A duke or duchess (female) can either be a monarch ruling over a duchy or a member of the nobility, historically of highest rank below the monarch. The title comes from French duc, itself from the Latin dux, 'leader', a term used in republican Rome to refer to a military commander without an official rank, and later coming to mean the leading military commander of a province. During the Middle Ages the title signified first among the Germanic monarchies.
Joan of Arc	Joan of Arc, nicknamed 'The Maid of Orléans', is a national heroine of France and a Roman Catholic saint. A peasant girl born in what is now eastern France, who claimed divine guidance, she led the French army to several important victories during the Hundred Years' War, which paved the way for the coronation of Charles VII. She was captured by the Burgundians, transferred to the English in exchange for money, put on trial by the pro-English Bishop of Beauvais Pierre Cauchon for charges of 'insubordination and heterodoxy,' and burned at the stake as a heretic when she was only 19 years old. Twenty-five years after the execution, an Inquisitorial court authorized by Pope Callixtus III examined the trial her innocent and declared her a martyr.
House of Commons	The House of Commons was the lower house of the National Assembly of the Republic of Korea during its Second Republic. The House of Commons was established by the Constitution of the Second Republic of Korea, which established a bicameral legislature.
Representative assembly	A representative assembly is a political institution in which a number of persons representing the population or privileged orders within the population of a state come together to debate, negotiate with the executive (originally the king or other ruler) and legislate. Examples in English-speaking countries are the United States Congress and the Parliament of the United Kingdom. The classical republics of Greece, Rome and Carthage included citizen assemblies (e.g. the Roman comitia).

12. The Crisis of the Late Middle Ages, 1300-1450

CHAPTER HIGHLIGHTS & NOTES: KEY TERMS, PEOPLE, PLACES, CONCEPTS

Avignon Papacy

The Avignon Papacy was the period from 1309 to 1376, during which seven successive popes resided in Avignon, in modern-day France, rather than in Rome. This situation arose from the conflict between the Papacy and the French crown.

Following the strife between Boniface VIII and Philip IV of France, and the death of his successor Benedict XI after only eight months in office, a deadlocked conclave finally elected Clement V, a Frenchman, as Pope in 1305. Clement declined to move to Rome, remaining in France, and in 1309 moved his court to the papal enclave at Avignon, where it remained for the next 67 years.

Babylonian captivity

The Babylonian captivity was the period in Jewish history during which the Jews of the ancient Kingdom of Judah were captives in Babylon--conventionally 587-538 BCE.

According to the Hebrew Bible, there were three deportations of Jews to Babylon: in 597 BCE, involving King Jeconiah and his court and many others; in 587/6 BCE, of his successor King Zedekiah and the rest of the people; and a possible deportation after the assassination of Gedaliah, the Babylonian-appointed governor of Yehud Province, possibly in 582 BCE. The forced exile ended in 538/7 BCE after the fall of Babylon to the Persian king Cyrus the Great, who gave the Jews permission to return to Yehud province and to rebuild the Temple.

The captivity and subsequent return to the Land of Israel and the rebuilding of the Second Temple in Jerusalem are considered significant events in Jewish history and culture, which had a far-reaching impact on the development of Judaism. Chronology

Table based on Rainer Albertz, 'Israel in exile: the history and literature of the sixth century BCE', p.xxi.

Catholic Church

The Catholic Church, is the world's largest Christian church. Headed by the Pope, it sees its mission as spreading the gospel of Christ, administering its sacraments and exercising charity.

The Catholic Church is one of the oldest religious institutions in the world and has played a prominent role in the history of Western civilisation.

Criticism

Criticism is the practice of judging the merits and faults of something or someone in an intelligible (or articulate) way. •The judger is called 'the critic'.•To engage in criticism is 'to criticize'.•One specific item of criticism is called 'a criticism'.

Criticism can be:•directed toward a person or an animal; at a group, authority or organization; at a specific behaviour; or at an object of some kind (an idea, a relationship, a condition, a process, or a thing).•personal (delivered directly from one person to another, in a personal capacity), or impersonal (expressing the view of an organization, and not aimed at anyone personally).•highly specific and detailed, or very abstract and general.•verbal (expressed in language) or non-verbal (expressed symbolically, or expressed through an action or a way of behaving).•explicit (the criticism is clearly stated) or implicit (a criticism is implied by what is being said, but it is not stated openly).•the result of critical thinking or spontaneous impulse.

To criticize does not necessarily imply 'to find fault', but the word is often taken to mean the simple expression of an objection against prejudice, or a disapproval. Often criticism involves active disagreement, but it may only mean 'taking sides'.

Council of Constance

The Council of Constance is the 16th ecumenical council recognized by the Roman Catholic Church, held from 1414 to 1418. The council ended the Three-Popes Controversy, by deposing or accepting the resignation of the remaining Papal claimants and electing Pope Martin V.

The Council also condemned and executed Jan Hus and ruled on issues of national sovereignty, the rights of pagans, and just war in response to a conflict between the Kingdom of Poland and the Order of the Teutonic Knights. The Council is important for its relationship to ecclesial Conciliarism and Papal supremacy. Origin and background

The council's main purpose was to end the Papal schism which had resulted from the confusion following the Avignon Papacy.

Hussite

The Hussites (Czech: Husité or Kališníci; 'Chalice People') were a Christian movement following the teachings of Czech reformer Jan Hus (c. 1369-1415), who became one of the forerunners of the Protestant Reformation. This predominantly religious movement was propelled by social issues and strengthened Czech national awareness.

After the Council of Constance lured Jan Hus in with a letter of indemnity.

University of Oxford

The University of Oxford is a university in Oxford, England. It is the second oldest surviving university in the world and the oldest in the English-speaking world. Although the exact date of its foundation remains unclear, there is evidence of teaching there as far back as the 11th century.

Antipope

An antipope is a person who, in opposition to the one who is generally seen as the legitimately elected Pope, makes a significantly accepted competing claim to be the Pope, the Bishop of Rome and leader of the Catholic Church.

Visit Cram101.com for full Practice Exams

At times between the 3rd and mid-15th century, antipopes were supported by a fairly significant faction of religious cardinals and secular kings and kingdoms. Persons who claim to be pope, but have few followers, such as the modern sedevacantist antipopes, are not classified with the historical antipopes.

Bridget of Sweden

Bridget of Sweden (1303 - 23 July 1373; also Birgitta of Vadstena, Saint Birgitta, was a mystic and saint, and founder of the Bridgettines nuns and monks after the death of her husband of twenty years. She was also the mother of Catherine of Vadstena.

She is one of the six patron saints of Europe, together with Benedict of Nursia, Saints Cyril and Methodius, Catherine of Siena and Edith Stein.

Jacquerie

The Jacquerie was a popular revolt in late medieval Europe by peasants that took place in northern France in the summer of 1358, during the Hundred Years' War. The revolt, which was violently suppressed after a few weeks of violence, centered in the Oise valley north of Paris. This rebellion became known as the Jacquerie because the nobles derided peasants as 'Jacques' or 'Jacques Bonhomme' for their padded surplice called 'jacque'.

John Ball

John Ball (c. 1338 - 15 July 1381) was an English Lollard priest who took a prominent part in the Peasants' Revolt of 1381. In that year, Ball gave a sermon in which he asked the rhetorical question, 'When Adam delved and Eve span, who was then the gentleman?'.

He was born and lived in St. Albans, Hertfordshire and subsequently at Colchester during the Black Death. He also lived in Kent at the time of the 1381 rebellion.

Society

A society, is a group of people related to each other through persistent relations, or a large social grouping sharing the same geographical or virtual territory, subject to the same political authority and dominant cultural expectations. Human societies are characterized by patterns of relationships (social relations) between individuals who share a distinctive culture and institutions; a given society may be described as the sum total of such relationships among its constituent members. In the social sciences, a larger society often evinces stratification and/or dominance patterns in subgroups.

Middle Ages

The Middle Ages is a stretch of European history that lasted from the 5th until the 15th centuries. It began with the collapse of the Western Roman Empire, and was followed by the Renaissance and the Age of Discovery. The Middle Ages is the middle period of the traditional division of Western history into Classical, Medieval, and Modern periods.

Divine Comedy

The Divine Comedy is an epic poem written by Dante Alighieri between 1308 and his death in 1321. It is widely considered the preeminent work of Italian literature, and is seen as one of the greatest works of world literature. The poem's imaginative and allegorical vision of the afterlife is a culmination of the medieval world-view as it had developed in the Western Church.

Visit Cram101.com for full Practice Exams

1. _________ is a zoonotic disease, circulating mainly among small rodents and their fleas, and is one of three types of infections caused by Yersinia pestis (formerly known as Pasteurella pestis), which belongs to the family Enterobacteriaceae. Without treatment, the _________ kills about two out of three infected humans within 4 days.

   The term _________ is derived from the Greek word bubo, meaning 'swollen gland'.

   a. Second Servile War
   b. Corporate crime
   c. Credit crisis of 1772
   d. Bubonic plague

2. _________ or Cantacuzenus was the Byzantine emperor from 1347 to 1354.

   Born in Constantinople, John Kantakouzenos was the son of Michael Kantakouzenos, governor of the Morea. Through his mother Theodora Palaiologina Angelina, he was a descendant of the reigning house of Palaiologos.

   a. John VI Kantakouzenos
   b. Lucius Tarquinius Superbus
   c. Wadysaw III Spindleshanks
   d. Second Servile War

3. The _________ was the lower house of the National Assembly of the Republic of Korea during its Second Republic. The _________ was established by the Constitution of the Second Republic of Korea, which established a bicameral legislature.

   a. Congress of Deputies
   b. House of Representatives
   c. Chamber of Deputies
   d. House of Commons

4. _________ (1303 - 23 July 1373; also Birgitta of Vadstena, Saint Birgitta, was a mystic and saint, and founder of the Bridgettines nuns and monks after the death of her husband of twenty years. She was also the mother of Catherine of Vadstena.

   She is one of the six patron saints of Europe, together with Benedict of Nursia, Saints Cyril and Methodius, Catherine of Siena and Edith Stein.

   a. Brother Lawrence
   b. Bruno of Cologne
   c. Bridget of Sweden
   d. Maria Orsola Bussone

5. . An _________ is a person who, in opposition to the one who is generally seen as the legitimately elected Pope, makes a significantly accepted competing claim to be the Pope, the Bishop of Rome and leader of the Catholic Church.

12. The Crisis of the Late Middle Ages, 1300-1450

CHAPTER QUIZ: KEY TERMS, PEOPLE, PLACES, CONCEPTS

At times between the 3rd and mid-15th century, _________s were supported by a fairly significant faction of religious cardinals and secular kings and kingdoms. Persons who claim to be pope, but have few followers, such as the modern sedevacantist _________s, are not classified with the historical _________s.

a. Papal infallibility
b. Erik the Red
c. Julia Antonia
d. Antipope

Visit Cram101.com for full Practice Exams

ANSWER KEY
12. The Crisis of the Late Middle Ages, 1300-1450

1. d
2. a
3. d
4. c
5. d

You can take the complete Chapter Practice Test

for 12. The Crisis of the Late Middle Ages, 1300-1450
on all key terms, persons, places, and concepts.

Online 99 Cents

http://www.epub141.56.21995.12.cram101.com/

Use www.Cram101.com for all your study needs

including Cram101's online interactive problem solving labs in

chemistry, statistics, mathematics, and more.

13. European Society in the Age of the Renaissance, 1350-1550

CHAPTER OUTLINE: KEY TERMS, PEOPLE, PLACES, CONCEPTS

- Renaissance
- Society
- Italian Renaissance
- Mantua
- Papal States
- Benvenuto Cellini
- Leon Battista Alberti
- Marsilio Ficino
- Giovanni Pico della Mirandola
- Virtus
- Civics
- Christian Church
- Aristotle
- Desiderius Erasmus
- Plutarch
- Bible
- Renaissance art
- Descent from the Cross
- Donatello
- Jan van Eyck
- Rogier van der Weyden

13. European Society in the Age of the Renaissance, 1350-1550

CHAPTER OUTLINE: KEY TERMS, PEOPLE, PLACES, CONCEPTS

- Genius
- Last Supper
- Mona Lisa
- Ark of the Covenant
- Burgundian
- Hundred Years' War
- Joan of Arc
- Catherine of Aragon
- Concordat of Bologna
- Iberian Peninsula
- House of Lancaster
- Granada
- Collection
- Converso
- Inquisition

Visit Cram101.com for full Practice Exams

Renaissance

The Renaissance was a cultural movement that spanned the period roughly from the 14th to the 17th century, beginning in Italy in the Late Middle Ages and later spreading to the rest of Europe. Though availability of paper and the invention of metal movable type sped the dissemination of ideas from the later 15th century, the changes of the Renaissance were not uniformly experienced across Europe.

As a cultural movement, it encompassed innovative flowering of Latin and vernacular literatures, beginning with the 14th-century resurgence of learning based on classical sources, which contemporaries credited to Petrarch, the development of linear perspective and other techniques of rendering a more natural reality in painting, and gradual but widespread educational reform.

Society

A society, is a group of people related to each other through persistent relations, or a large social grouping sharing the same geographical or virtual territory, subject to the same political authority and dominant cultural expectations. Human societies are characterized by patterns of relationships (social relations) between individuals who share a distinctive culture and institutions; a given society may be described as the sum total of such relationships among its constituent members. In the social sciences, a larger society often evinces stratification and/or dominance patterns in subgroups.

Italian Renaissance

The Italian Renaissance was the earliest manifestation of the general European Renaissance, a period of great cultural change and achievement that began in Italy during the 14th century and lasted until the 16th century, marking the transition between Medieval and Early Modern Europe. The term Renaissance is in essence a modern one that came into currency in the 19th century, in the work of historians such as Jules Michelet and Jacob Burckhardt. Although the origins of a movement that was confined largely to the literate culture of intellectual endeavor and patronage can be traced to the earlier part of the 14th century, many aspects of Italian culture and society remained largely Medieval; the Renaissance did not come into full swing until the end of the century.

Mantua

A mantua is an article of women's clothing worn in the late 17th century and 18th century. Originally a loose gown, the later mantua was an overgown or robe typically worn over stays, stomacher and a co-ordinating petticoat.

The earliest mantuas emerged in the late 17th century as a comfortable alternative to the boned bodices and separate skirts then widely worn.

Papal States

The Papal States were territories in the Italian peninsula under the sovereign direct rule of the Pope, from the 500s until 1870. They were among the major states of Italy from roughly the sixth century until the Italian peninsula was unified in 1861 by the Kingdom of Piedmont-Sardinia. After 1861 the Papal States, in less territorially extensive form, continued to exist until 1870. At their most extensive they covered most of the modern Italian regions of Romagna, Marche, Umbria and Lazio.

Visit Cram101.com for full Practice Exams

13. European Society in the Age of the Renaissance, 1350-1550

Benvenuto Cellini	Benvenuto Cellini was an Italian goldsmith, sculptor, painter, soldier and musician, who also wrote a famous autobiography. He was one of the most important artists of Mannerism. Biography Youth Benvenuto Cellini was born in Florence, Italy.
Leon Battista Alberti	Leon Battista Alberti was an Italian author, artist, architect, poet, priest, linguist, philosopher, cryptographer and general Renaissance humanist polymath. Although he is often characterized as an 'architect' exclusively, as James Beck has observed, 'to single out one of Leon Battista's 'fields' over others as somehow functionally independent and self-sufficient is of no help at all to any effort to characterize Leon Battista Alberti's extensive explorations in the fine arts.' Leon Battista Alberti's life was described in Giorgio Vasari's Vite de' più eccellenti pittori, scultori, e architettori or 'Lives of the most excellent painters, sculptors and architects'. Childhood and education An Italian humanist, Leon Battista Alberti is often seen as a model of the Renaissance 'universal man'.
Marsilio Ficino	Marsilio Ficino was one of the most influential humanist philosophers of the early Italian Renaissance, an astrologer, a reviver of Neoplatonism who was in touch with every major academic thinker and writer of his day, and the first translator of Plato's complete extant works into Latin. His Florentine Academy, an attempt to revive Plato's school, had enormous influence on the direction and tenor of the Italian Renaissance and the development of European philosophy. Marsilio Ficino was born at Figline Valdarno.
Giovanni Pico della Mirandola	Count Giovanni Pico della Mirandola was an Italian Renaissance philosopher. He is famed for the events of 1486, when at the age of 23, he proposed to defend 900 theses on religion, philosophy, natural philosophy and magic against all comers, for which he wrote the famous Oration on the Dignity of Man, which has been called the 'Manifesto of the Renaissance', and a key text of Renaissance humanism and of what has been called the 'Hermetic Reformation.' Family Giovanni was born at Mirandola, near Modena, the youngest son of Francesco I, Lord of Mirandola and Count of Concordia (1415-1467), by his wife Giulia, daughter of Feltrino Boiardo, Count di Scandiano. The family had long dwelt in the Castle of Mirandola (Duchy of Modena), which had become independent in the fourteenth century and had received in 1414 from the Emperor Sigismund the fief of Concordia.
Virtus	In Roman mythology, Virtus was the deity of bravery and military strength, the personification of the Roman virtue of virtus. The Greek equivalent deity was Arete.

Civics	Civics is the study of rights and duties of citizenship. In other words, it is the study of government with attention to the role of citizens ? as opposed to external factors ? in the operation and oversight of government. Within a given political or ethical tradition, civics refers to educating the citizens.
Christian Church	The Christian Church is the assembly or association of followers of Jesus Christ. The Greek term ? κκλησ?α, which in its appearances in the New Testament is usually translated as 'church', basically means 'assembly'. The term appears in two verses of the canonical Gospel of Matthew, twenty-four verses of the Acts of the Apostles, fifty-eight verses of the letters of Paul the Apostle (including the earliest instances of its use in relation to a Christian body), two verses of the Letter to the Hebrews, one verse of the Epistle of James, three verses of the Third Epistle of John, and nineteen verses of the Book of Revelation.
Aristotle	Aristotle (384 BC - 322 BC) was a Greek philosopher and polymath, a student of Plato and teacher of Alexander the Great. His writings cover many subjects, including physics, metaphysics, poetry, theater, music, logic, rhetoric, linguistics, politics, government, ethics, biology, and zoology. Together with Plato and Socrates (Plato's teacher), Aristotle is one of the most important founding figures in Western philosophy.
Desiderius Erasmus	Desiderius Erasmus Roterodamus (October 28, 1466 - July 12, 1536), sometimes known as Desiderius Erasmus of Rotterdam, was a Dutch Renaissance humanist and a Catholic priest and theologian. His scholarly name Desiderius Erasmus Roterodamus comprises the following three elements: the Latin noun desiderium ; the Greek adjective ?ρ?σμιος (erásmios) meaning 'desired', and, in the form Erasmus, also the name of a St. Erasmus of Formiae; and the Latinized adjectival form for the city of Rotterdam (Roterodamus = 'of Rotterdam'). Erasmus was a classical scholar who wrote in a 'pure' Latin style and enjoyed the sobriquet 'Prince of the Humanists.' He has been called 'the crowning glory of the Christian humanists.' Using humanist techniques for working on texts, he prepared important new Latin and Greek editions of the New Testament.
Plutarch	Plutarch, born Plutarchos then named, on his becoming a Roman citizen, Lucius Mestrius Plutarchus , c. 46 - 120 CE, was a Greek historian, biographer, essayist, and Middle Platonist known primarily for his Parallel Lives and Moralia. He was born to a prominent family in Chaeronea, Boeotia, a town about twenty miles east of Delphi. Early life Plutarch was born in 46 CE in the small town of Chaeronea, in the Greek region known as Boeotia.

13. European Society in the Age of the Renaissance, 1350-1550

CHAPTER HIGHLIGHTS & NOTES: KEY TERMS, PEOPLE, PLACES, CONCEPTS

Bible	The Bible is the various collections of sacred scripture of the various branches of Judaism and Christianity. The Bible, in its various editions, is the best-selling book in history. There is no single Bible, and both the individual books (Biblical canon), their contents and their order vary between denominations.
Renaissance art	Renaissance art is the painting, sculpture and decorative arts of that period of European history known as the Renaissance, emerging as a distinct style in Italy in about 1400, in parallel with developments which occurred in philosophy, literature, music and science. Renaissance art, perceived as a 'rebirth' of ancient traditions, took as its foundation the art of Classical antiquity, but transformed that tradition by the absorption of recent developments in the art of Northern Europe and by application of contemporary scientific knowledge. Renaissance art, with Renaissance Humanist philosophy, spread throughout Europe, affecting both artists and their patrons with the development of new techniques and new artistic sensibilities.
Descent from the Cross	The Descent from the Cross, is the scene, as depicted in art, from the Gospels' accounts of Joseph of Arimathea and Nicodemus taking Christ down from the cross after his crucifixion (John 19:38-42). In Byzantine art the topic became popular in the 9th century, and in the West from the 10th century. The Descent from the Cross is the 13th Station of the Cross.
Donatello	Donato di Niccolò di Betto Bardi (circa 1386 - December 13, 1466), also known as Donatello, was an early Renaissance Italian artist and sculptor from Florence. He is, in part, known for his work in bas-relief, a form of shallow relief sculpture that, in Donatello's case, incorporated significant 15th century developments in perspectival illusionism. Early life Donatello was the son of Niccolò di Betto Bardi, who was a member of the Florentine Wool Combers Guild, and was born in Florence, most likely in the year 1386. Donatello was educated in the house of the Martelli family.
Jan van Eyck	Jan van Eyck was a Flemish painter active in Bruges and is generally considered one of the most significant Northern European painters of the 15th century. The few surviving records indicate that he was born around 1390, most likely in Maaseik. Outside of works completed with his brother Hubert van Eyck and those ascribed to Hand G -believed to be Jan- of the Turin-Milan Hours illuminated manuscript, only about 23 surviving works are confidentaly attributed to him, of which ten, including the Ghent altarpiece, are signed and dated.
Rogier van der Weyden	Rogier van der Weyden or Roger de la Pasture was an Early Flemish painter. His surviving works consist mainly of religious triptychs, altarpieces and commissioned single and diptych portraits.

Genius

In ancient Roman religion, the genius was the individual instance of a general divine nature that is present in every individual person, place or thing.

Religious context

Classical polytheism--that is, the religions of the peoples within the Graeco-Roman domain from before the beginning of alphabetic writing in the Mediterranean lands to the rise of Christianity--embraced a universal divine nature, the belief in which is still being investigated whether under the name polytheism or paganism. As the theologian Paul Tillich pointed out, polytheism was never as simple as a belief in multiple gods.

Last Supper

After Luther's objections to large public religious images had started to fade, Lucas Cranach the Elder, along with his son and workshop began to work on a number of altarpieces of the Last Supper, among other subjects.

In some such depictions Christ is shown with the traditional halo, but the apostles are represented as leading reformers, without halos. The altarpiece of the main church in Martin Luther's home of Wittenberg has a traditional representation of the Last Supper in the main panel, except that the apostle having a drink poured is a portrait of Luther, and the server may be one of Cranach.

Mona Lisa

The Mona Lisa is a half-length portrait of a woman by the Italian artist Leonardo da Vinci, which has been acclaimed as 'the best known, the most visited, the most written about, the most sung about, the most parodied work of art in the world.'

The painting, thought to be a portrait of Mona Lisa Gherardini, the wife of Francesco del Giocondo, is in oil on a poplar panel, and is believed to have been painted between 1503 and 1506. It was acquired by King Francis I of France and is now the property of the French Republic, on permanent display at the Musée du Louvre in Paris since 1797. The ambiguity of the subject's expression, which is frequently described as enigmatic, the monumentality of the composition, the subtle modeling of forms and the atmospheric illusionism were novel qualities that have contributed to the continuing fascination and study of the work. Title and subject

The title of the painting that is known in English as Mona Lisa stems from a description by Renaissance art historian Giorgio Vasari, who wrote 'Leonardo undertook to paint, for Francesco del Giocondo, the portrait of Mona Lisa, his wife.' Mona in Italian is a polite form of address originating as ma donna -similar to Ma'am, Madam, or my lady in English. This became madonna, and its contraction mona.

Ark of the Covenant

The Ark of the Covenant is a biblical vessel, described in (1 Kings 8:9) as solely containing the Tablets of Stone on which the Ten Commandments were inscribed. According to Hebrews 9:4 and some traditional interpretations of Exodus 16:33-34 and Numbers 17:25-26, the Ark also contained Aaron's rod and a jar of manna.

Visit Cram101.com for full Practice Exams

CHAPTER HIGHLIGHTS & NOTES: KEY TERMS, PEOPLE, PLACES, CONCEPTS

Burgundian

The Burgundian party was a political allegiance in France that formed during the reign of Charles VI during the latter half of the Hundred Years' War. During that era the term 'Burgundian' also applied to loyal subjects of the dukes of Burgundy.

The Dukes of Burgundy had inherited a large number of lands scattered from what is now the border of Switzerland up to the North Sea.

Hundred Years' War

The Hundred Years' War was a series of wars waged from 1337 to 1453 by the House of Valois and the House of Plantagenet, also known as the House of Anjou, for the French throne, which had become vacant upon the extinction of the senior Capetian line of French kings. The House of Valois claimed the title of King of France, while the Plantagenets claimed the thrones of both France and England. The Plantagenet kings were the 12th-century rulers of the kingdom of England, and had their roots in the French regions of Anjou and Normandy.

Joan of Arc

Joan of Arc, nicknamed 'The Maid of Orléans', is a national heroine of France and a Roman Catholic saint. A peasant girl born in what is now eastern France, who claimed divine guidance, she led the French army to several important victories during the Hundred Years' War, which paved the way for the coronation of Charles VII. She was captured by the Burgundians, transferred to the English in exchange for money, put on trial by the pro-English Bishop of Beauvais Pierre Cauchon for charges of 'insubordination and heterodoxy,' and burned at the stake as a heretic when she was only 19 years old.

Twenty-five years after the execution, an Inquisitorial court authorized by Pope Callixtus III examined the trial her innocent and declared her a martyr.

Catherine of Aragon

Catherine of Aragon also known as Katherine or Katharine, was Queen of England as the first wife of King Henry VIII of England and Princess of Wales as the wife to Arthur, Prince of Wales. In 1507, she also held the position of Ambassador for the Spanish Court in England when her father found himself without one, becoming the first female ambassador in European history. For six months, she served as regent of England while Henry VIII was in France.

Concordat of Bologna

The Concordat of Bologna marking a stage in the evolution of the Gallican Church, was an agreement between King Francis I of France and Pope Leo X that Francis negotiated in the wake of his victory at Marignano in September 1515. The groundwork was laid in a series of personal meetings of king and pope in Bologna, 11-15 December 1515. The concordat was signed in Rome on 18 August 1516.

The Concordat explicitly superseded the Pragmatic Sanction of Bourges, (1438), which had proved ineffective in guaranteeing the privileges of the Church in France, where bishoprics and abbacies had been wrangled over even before the Parlement of Paris: 'hardly anywhere were elections held in due form', R. Aubenas observes, 'for the king succeeded in foisting his own candidates upon the electors by every conceivable means, not excluding the most ruthless.'

Visit Cram101.com for full Practice Exams

The Concordat permitted the Pope to collect all the income that the Catholic Church made in France, while the King of France was confirmed in his right to tithe the clerics and to restrict their right of appeal to Rome. The Concordat confirmed the King of France's right to nominate appointments to benefices-archbishops, bishops, abbots and priors- enabling the Crown, by controlling its personnel, to decide who was to lead the Gallican Church.

Iberian Peninsula

The Iberian Peninsula, commonly called Iberia, is a peninsula located in the extreme southwest of Europe and includes the modern-day sovereign states of Spain, Portugal, Andorra and France, as well as the British Overseas Territory of Gibraltar. It is the westernmost of the three major southern European peninsulas-the Iberian, Italian, and Balkan peninsulas. It is bordered on the southeast and east by the Mediterranean Sea, and on the north, west and southwest by the Atlantic Ocean.

House of Lancaster

The House of Lancaster was a cadet branch of the royal House of Plantagenet. It was one of the opposing factions involved in the Wars of the Roses, an intermittent dynastic struggle which affected England and Wales during the 15th century. The family provided England with three kings: Henry IV of England, who ruled 1399-1413; Henry V of England, who ruled 1413-1422; and Henry VI of England and (II of) France, who ruled 1422-1461 and 1470-1471. The term 'Lancastrian' refers to members of the family as well as their supporters.

Granada

Granada is a 2009 German-style board game developed by Dirk Henn and published by Queen Games. It is based on and heavily inspired by Henn's earlier game, the Spiel des Jahres-winning Alhambra. Due to its similar theme, it is published as a 'standalone game in the Alhambra family'.

Collection

A museum is distinguished by a collection of often unique objects that forms the core of its activities for exhibitions, education, research, etc. This differentiates it from an archive or library, where the contents may be more paper-based, replaceable and less exhibition oriented. A museum normally has a collecting policy for new acquisitions, so only objects in certain categories and of a certain quality are accepted into the collection.

Converso

A converso and its feminine form conversa was a Jew or Muslim who converted to Catholicism in Spain or Portugal, particularly during the 14th and 15th centuries, or one of their descendents. Mass conversions once took place under significant government pressure. The Treaty of Granada (1491) at the last surrender of Al-Andalus issued clear protections of religious rights; the Alhambra Decree (1492) began the reversal.

Inquisition

The Inquisition was a group of institutions within the judicial system of the Roman Catholic Church whose aim was to 'fight against heretics'. It started in 12th-century France to combat the spread of heresy and error, and was later expanded to other European countries, as well as throughout the Spanish and Portuguese empires in the Americas, Asia and Africa.

Visit Cram101.com for full Practice Exams

13. European Society in the Age of the Renaissance, 1350-1550

CHAPTER HIGHLIGHTS & NOTES: KEY TERMS, PEOPLE, PLACES, CONCEPTS

Historical phases of the Inquisition include: the Medieval Inquisition; the Spanish Inquisition; the Portuguese Inquisition; and the Roman Inquisition.

The term Inquisition can apply to any one of several institutions which fought against heretics within the justice system of the Roman Catholic Church.

CHAPTER QUIZ: KEY TERMS, PEOPLE, PLACES, CONCEPTS

1. The _________ was a series of wars waged from 1337 to 1453 by the House of Valois and the House of Plantagenet, also known as the House of Anjou, for the French throne, which had become vacant upon the extinction of the senior Capetian line of French kings. The House of Valois claimed the title of King of France, while the Plantagenets claimed the thrones of both France and England. The Plantagenet kings were the 12th-century rulers of the kingdom of England, and had their roots in the French regions of Anjou and Normandy.

   a. Dual monarchy of England and France
   b. Cagot
   c. Hundred Years' War
   d. Charte d'Alaon

2. Count _________ was an Italian Renaissance philosopher. He is famed for the events of 1486, when at the age of 23, he proposed to defend 900 theses on religion, philosophy, natural philosophy and magic against all comers, for which he wrote the famous Oration on the Dignity of Man, which has been called the 'Manifesto of the Renaissance', and a key text of Renaissance humanism and of what has been called the 'Hermetic Reformation.' Family

   Giovanni was born at Mirandola, near Modena, the youngest son of Francesco I, Lord of Mirandola and Count of Concordia (1415-1467), by his wife Giulia, daughter of Feltrino Boiardo, Count di Scandiano. The family had long dwelt in the Castle of Mirandola (Duchy of Modena), which had become independent in the fourteenth century and had received in 1414 from the Emperor Sigismund the fief of Concordia.

   a. Gaetano da Thiene
   b. Pietro Pomponazzi
   c. Giovanni Pico della Mirandola
   d. Erik the Red

3. . The _________ was a cultural movement that spanned the period roughly from the 14th to the 17th century, beginning in Italy in the Late Middle Ages and later spreading to the rest of Europe.

Though availability of paper and the invention of metal movable type sped the dissemination of ideas from the later 15th century, the changes of the _________ were not uniformly experienced across Europe.

As a cultural movement, it encompassed innovative flowering of Latin and vernacular literatures, beginning with the 14th-century resurgence of learning based on classical sources, which contemporaries credited to Petrarch, the development of linear perspective and other techniques of rendering a more natural reality in painting, and gradual but widespread educational reform.

a. Second Thirty Years' War
b. Space Age
c. The long peace
d. Renaissance

4. The _________ were territories in the Italian peninsula under the sovereign direct rule of the Pope, from the 500s until 1870. They were among the major states of Italy from roughly the sixth century until the Italian peninsula was unified in 1861 by the Kingdom of Piedmont-Sardinia. After 1861 the _________, in less territorially extensive form, continued to exist until 1870. At their most extensive they covered most of the modern Italian regions of Romagna, Marche, Umbria and Lazio. This was commonly called the temporal power of the Pope, as opposed to his ecclesiastical primacy.

a. Symmachean forgeries
b. Second Servile War
c. Baptism of Poland
d. Papal States

5. The _________ is the various collections of sacred scripture of the various branches of Judaism and Christianity. The _________, in its various editions, is the best-selling book in history.

There is no single _________, and both the individual books (Biblical canon), their contents and their order vary between denominations.

a. Personal god
b. Bible
c. Biblical canon
d. Binding and loosing

Visit Cram101.com for full Practice Exams

ANSWER KEY

13. European Society in the Age of the Renaissance, 1350-1550

---

1. c

2. c

3. d

4. d

5. b

You can take the complete Chapter Practice Test

for 13. European Society in the Age of the Renaissance, 1350-1550

on all key terms, persons, places, and concepts.

Online 99 Cents

http://www.epub141.56.21995.13.cram101.com/

Use www.Cram101.com for all your study needs

including Cram101's online interactive problem solving labs in

chemistry, statistics, mathematics, and more.

14. Reformations and Religious Wars, 1500-1600

CHAPTER OUTLINE: KEY TERMS, PEOPLE, PLACES, CONCEPTS

- Christian Church
- Religious violence
- Religious war
- Bishop
- Criticism
- Martin Luther
- Purgatory
- Salvation
- Johann Eck
- Ten Commandments
- Eucharist
- Lutheranism
- Protestantism
- Radical Reformation
- Sacrament
- Anabaptist
- Church
- Holy Roman Empire
- Peace of Augsburg
- Protestant Reformation
- Anne Boleyn

CHAPTER OUTLINE: KEY TERMS, PEOPLE, PLACES, CONCEPTS

Catherine of Aragon

Thomas Cromwell

Sexual Division of Labor

Catholicism

Christianity

Puritan

Thomas Cranmer

Mary, Queen of Scots

Spanish Armada

Huguenot

John Knox

Counter-Reformation

Stanislaus Hosius

Eastern Europe

Council of Trent

Desiderius Erasmus

Inquisition

Papal States

Roman Inquisition

Church of Scotland

Ignatius of Loyola

14. Reformations and Religious Wars, 1500-1600

CHAPTER OUTLINE: KEY TERMS, PEOPLE, PLACES, CONCEPTS

______ Carmelites

______ Catherine de' Medici

______ Concordat of Bologna

______ Edict of Nantes

______ Politique

______ Union of Utrecht

______ Abdication

______ Religious persecution

CHAPTER HIGHLIGHTS & NOTES: KEY TERMS, PEOPLE, PLACES, CONCEPTS

Christian Church

The Christian Church is the assembly or association of followers of Jesus Christ. The Greek term ?κκλησ?α, which in its appearances in the New Testament is usually translated as 'church', basically means 'assembly'. The term appears in two verses of the canonical Gospel of Matthew, twenty-four verses of the Acts of the Apostles, fifty-eight verses of the letters of Paul the Apostle (including the earliest instances of its use in relation to a Christian body), two verses of the Letter to the Hebrews, one verse of the Epistle of James, three verses of the Third Epistle of John, and nineteen verses of the Book of Revelation.

Religious violence

Religious violence is a term that covers phenomena where religion, in its diversity, is either the subject or object of violent behaviour. Religious violence is, specifically, violence that is motivated by or in reaction to religious precepts, texts, or doctrines. This includes violence against religious institutions, persons, objects, or when the violence is motivated to some degree by some religious aspect of the target or precept of the attacker.

Religious war

A religious war is a war caused by, or justified by, religious differences. It can involve one state with an established religion against another state with a different religion or a different sect within the same religion, or a religiously motivated group attempting to spread its faith by violence, or to suppress another group because of its religious beliefs or practices.

Bishop

In the Catholic Church, a bishop is an ordained minister who holds the fullness of the sacrament of Holy Orders and is responsible for teaching doctrine, governing Catholics in his jurisdiction, and sanctifying the world and for representing the Church. Catholics trace the origins of the office of bishop to the apostles, who were endowed with a special charism by the Holy Spirit at Pentecost. Catholics believe this special charism has been transmitted through an unbroken succession of bishops by the laying on of hands in the sacrament of Holy Orders.

Criticism

Criticism is the practice of judging the merits and faults of something or someone in an intelligible (or articulate) way. •The judger is called 'the critic'.•To engage in criticism is 'to criticize'.•One specific item of criticism is called 'a criticism'.

Criticism can be:•directed toward a person or an animal; at a group, authority or organization; at a specific behaviour; or at an object of some kind (an idea, a relationship, a condition, a process, or a thing).•personal (delivered directly from one person to another, in a personal capacity), or impersonal (expressing the view of an organization, and not aimed at anyone personally).•highly specific and detailed, or very abstract and general.•verbal (expressed in language) or non-verbal (expressed symbolically, or expressed through an action or a way of behaving).•explicit (the criticism is clearly stated) or implicit (a criticism is implied by what is being said, but it is not stated openly).•the result of critical thinking or spontaneous impulse.

To criticize does not necessarily imply 'to find fault', but the word is often taken to mean the simple expression of an objection against prejudice, or a disapproval. Often criticism involves active disagreement, but it may only mean 'taking sides'.

Martin Luther

Martin Luther was a German monk, former Catholic priest, professor of theology and seminal figure of a reform movement in sixteenth century Christianity, subsequently known as the Protestant Reformation. He strongly disputed the claim that freedom from God's punishment for sin could be purchased with money. He confronted indulgence salesman Johann Tetzel with his Ninety-Five Theses in 1517. His refusal to retract all of his writings at the demand of Pope Leo X in 1520 and the Holy Roman Emperor Charles V at the Diet of Worms in 1521 resulted in his excommunication by the pope and condemnation as an outlaw by the Emperor.

Purgatory

Purgatory is the condition or process of purification or temporary punishment in which, it is believed, the souls of those who die in a state of grace are made ready for Heaven. This is an idea that has ancient roots and is well-attested in early Christian literature, while the conception of purgatory as a geographically situated place is largely the creation of medieval Christian piety and imagination.

The notion of purgatory is associated particularly with the Latin Rite of the Catholic Church (in the Eastern sui juris churches or rites it is a doctrine, though often without using the name 'Purgatory'); Anglicans of the Anglo-Catholic tradition generally also hold to the belief.

Salvation

The branch of Christian theology that deals with salvation and redemption is called Soteriology. It is derived from Greek soterion (salvation) (from soter 'savior, redeemer') + English -logy.

Speaking only within the scope of Christian theology in this article, soteriology examines the role of Jesus Christ as saviour, and redeemer.

Johann Eck

Dr. Johann Maier von Johann Eck was a German Scholastic theologian and defender of Catholicism during the Protestant Reformation. Johann Eck argued that the beliefs of Martin Luther and Jan Hus were similar.

Johann Eck was born Johann Maier at Johann Eck in Swabia, and derived his additional surname from his birthplace, which he himself, after 1505, always modified into Johann Eckius or Eccius, i.e. 'of Johann Eck.' His father, Michael Maier, was a peasant and bailiff, or Amtmann, of the village.

Ten Commandments

The Ten Commandments, is a list of religious and moral imperatives that, according to the Hebrew Bible, were given by God to the people of Israel from the mountain referred to as Mount Sinai or Horeb. The Bible describes their form as being spoken by God and subsequently as an inscription on two stone tablets which God wrote with his finger, after which God gave the tablets to Moses. The Ten Commandments are recognized as a moral foundation in Judaism and Christianity.

Eucharist

The Eucharist, Sacrament of the Altar, the Blessed Sacrament, or The Lord's Supper, and other names, is a Christian sacrament or ordinance, generally considered to be a re-enactment of the Last Supper, the final meal that Jesus Christ shared with his disciples before his arrest and crucifixion, during which he gave them bread, saying, 'This is my body', and wine, saying, 'This is my blood'.

There are different interpretations of the significance of the Eucharist, but 'there is more of a consensus among Christians about the meaning of the Eucharist than would appear from the confessional debates over the sacramental presence, the effects of the Eucharist, and the proper auspices under which it may be celebrated.'

The phrase 'the Eucharist' may refer not only to the rite but also to the consecrated bread (leavened or unleavened) and wine or, unfermented grape juice (in some Protestant denominations) or water (in Mormonism), used in the rite, and, in this sense, communicants may speak of 'receiving the Eucharist', as well as 'celebrating the Eucharist'.

Names and their origin

Eucharist, from Greek ε?χαριστ?α (eucharistia), means 'thanksgiving'.

Lutheranism

Lutheranism is a major branch of Western Christianity that identifies with the theology of Martin Luther, a German reformer.

Luther's efforts to reform the theology and practice of the Roman Catholic Church launched the Protestant Reformation. Beginning with the 95 Theses, Luther's writings were disseminated internationally, spreading the ideas of the Reformation beyond the ability of governmental and churchly authorities to control it.

Protestantism

Protestantism is one of the major groupings within Christianity. It has been defined as 'any of several church denominations denying the universal authority of the Pope and affirming the Reformation principles of justification by faith alone, the priesthood of all believers, and the primacy of the Bible as the only source of revealed truth' and, more broadly, to mean Christianity outside 'of a Catholic or Eastern church'. It is a movement that began in Germany in the early 16th century as a reaction against medieval Roman Catholic doctrines and practices, especially in regards to salvation, justification, and ecclesiology.

Radical Reformation

The Radical Reformation was a 16th century response to what was believed to be the corruption in both the Roman Catholic Church and the expanding Magisterial Protestant movement led by Martin Luther and many others. Beginning in Germany and Switzerland, the Radical Reformation birthed many radical Protestant groups throughout Europe. The term covers both radical reformers like Thomas Müntzer, Andreas Karlstadt, groups like the Zwickau prophets and anabaptist groups like the Hutterites and the Mennonites.

Sacrament

In The Church of Jesus Christ of Latter-day Saints (LDS Church, commonly called Mormons), the Holy Sacrament of the Lord's Supper, most often simply referred to as the sacrament, is the sacrament in which participants partake of bread and drink water in remembrance of the body and blood of Jesus Christ. It is similar in some ways, but different in others to the Eucharist in the Catholic Church, or communion or the Lord's Supper in other Christian denominations. Normally in LDS congregations, the sacrament is provided every Sunday as part of the sacrament meeting.

Anabaptist

Anabaptists are Christians of the Radical Reformation of 16th-century Europe, considered Protestant by some, although some consider Anabaptism to be a distinct movement from Protestantism. The Amish, Hutterites, and Mennonites are direct descendants of the movement.

The name Anabaptist is derived from the Greek term anabaptista, or 'one who baptizes over again.' This name was given them by their enemies in reference to the practice of 're-baptizing' converts who 'already had been baptized' as infants.

Church

In the Christian religion, a church is a building or structure to facilitate the meeting of its members. Originally, Jewish Christians met in synagogues, such as the Cenacle, and in one another's homes, known as house churches. As Christianity grew and became more accepted by governments, notably with the Edict of Milan, rooms and, eventually, entire buildings were set aside for the explicit purpose of Christian worship, such as the Church of the Holy Sepulcher.

Visit Cram101.com for full Practice Exams

14. Reformations and Religious Wars, 1500-1600

CHAPTER HIGHLIGHTS & NOTES: KEY TERMS, PEOPLE, PLACES, CONCEPTS

Holy Roman Empire	The Holy Roman Empire was a varying complex of lands that existed from 962 to 1806 in Central Europe. It grew out of East Francia, one of the primary divisions of the Frankish Empire. Its character changed during the Middle Ages and the Early Modern period, when the power of the emperor gradually weakened in favour of the princes.
Peace of Augsburg	The Peace of Augsburg, was a treaty between Charles V and the forces of the Schmalkaldic League, an alliance of Lutheran princes, on September 25, 1555, at the imperial city of Augsburg, now in present-day Bavaria, Germany. It officially ended the religious struggle between the two groups and made the legal division of Christendom permanent within the Holy Roman Empire. The Peace established the principle Cuius regio, eius religio, which allowed Holy Roman Empire's states' princes to select either Lutheranism or Catholicism within the domains they controlled, ultimately reaffirming the independence they had over their states.
Protestant Reformation	The Protestant Reformation was the 16th-century schism within Western Christianity initiated by Martin Luther, John Calvin and other early Protestants. It was sparked by the 1517 posting of Luther's Ninety-Five Theses. The efforts of the self-described 'reformers', who objected to ('protested') the doctrines, rituals, leadership and ecclesiastical structure of the Roman Catholic Church, led to the creation of new national Protestant churches.
Anne Boleyn	Anne Boleyn; c.1501/1507 - 19 May 1536) was Queen of England from 1533 to 1536 as the second wife of Henry VIII of England and Marquess of Pembroke in her own right. Henry's marriage to Anne, and her subsequent execution, made her a key figure in the political and religious upheaval that was the start of the English Reformation. A commoner, Anne was the daughter of Thomas Boleyn, 1st Earl of Wiltshire and his wife, Lady Elizabeth Howard, and was educated in the Netherlands and France, largely as a maid of honour to Claude of France.
Catherine of Aragon	Catherine of Aragon also known as Katherine or Katharine, was Queen of England as the first wife of King Henry VIII of England and Princess of Wales as the wife to Arthur, Prince of Wales. In 1507, she also held the position of Ambassador for the Spanish Court in England when her father found himself without one, becoming the first female ambassador in European history. For six months, she served as regent of England while Henry VIII was in France.
Thomas Cromwell	Thomas Cromwell, 1st Earl of Essex, was an English lawyer and statesman who served as chief minister to King Henry VIII of England from 1532 to 1540. Thomas Cromwell was one of the strongest advocates of the English Reformation. He helped engineer an annulment of the King's marriage to Catherine of Aragon, so that Henry could marry his mistress Anne Boleyn.

Sexual Division of Labor	The Sexual Division of Labor is defined as the delegation of different tasks between males and females. Among human foragers, males and females target different types of foods and share them with each other for a mutual or familial benefit. In some species, males and females eat slightly different foods, while in other species, males and females will routinely share food-but only in humans are these two attributes combined.
Catholicism	Catholicism is a broad term for the body of the Catholic faith, its theologies and doctrines, its liturgical, ethical, spiritual, and behavioral characteristics, as well as a religious people as a whole. For many the term usually refers to Christians and churches belonging to the Roman Catholic Church in full communion with the Holy See. For others it refers to the churches of the first millennium, including, besides the Roman Catholic Church, the Eastern Orthodox Church, the Oriental Orthodox Church, and the Assyrian Church of the East.
Christianity	Christianity is a monotheistic and Abrahamic religion based on the life and teachings of Jesus Christ as presented in canonical gospels and other New Testament writings. Most adherents of the Christian faith, known as Christians, believe that Jesus is the Son of God, fully divine and fully human and the savior of humanity prophesied in the Old Testament. Consequentially, Christians commonly refer to Jesus as Christ or Messiah.
Puritan	The Puritans were a significant grouping of English Protestants in the 16th and 17th centuries, including, but not limited to, English Calvinists. Puritanism in this sense was founded by some Marian exiles from the clergy shortly after the accession of Elizabeth I of England in 1558, as an activist movement within the Church of England. The designation 'Puritan' is often incorrectly used, notably based on the assumption that hedonism and puritanism are antonyms.
Thomas Cranmer	Thomas Cranmer was a leader of the English Reformation and Archbishop of Canterbury during the reigns of Henry VIII, Edward VI and, for a short time, Mary I. He helped build a favourable case for Henry's divorce from Catherine of Aragon which resulted in the separation of the English Church from union with the Holy See. Along with Thomas Cromwell, he supported the principle of Royal Supremacy, in which the king was considered sovereign over the Church within his realm. During Cranmer's tenure as Archbishop of Canterbury, he was responsible for establishing the first doctrinal and liturgical structures of the reformed Church of England.
Mary, Queen of Scots	Mary, Queen of Scots, was queen regnant of Scotland from 14 December 1542 to 24 July 1567 and queen consort of France from 10 July 1559 to 5 December 1560. Mary, the only surviving legitimate child of King James V of Scotland, was 6 days old when her father died and she succeeded to the throne.

14. Reformations and Religious Wars, 1500-1600

Spanish Armada

The Spanish Armada was the Spanish fleet that sailed against England under the command of the Duke of Medina Sidonia in 1588, with the intention of overthrowing Elizabeth I of England and putting an end to her involvement in the Spanish Netherlands and in privateering in the Atlantic and Pacific.

The Armada reached and anchored outside Gravelines, but, while awaiting communications from Parma's army, it was driven out by an English fire ship attack. In the ensuing battle, the Spanish fleet was forced to abandon its rendezvous.

Huguenot

The Huguenots were members of the Protestant Reformed Church of France during the 16th and 17th centuries. French Protestants were inspired by the writings of John Calvin in the 1530s, and they were called Huguenots by the 1560s. By the end of the 17th century and into the 18th century, roughly 500,000 Huguenots had fled France during a series of religious persecutions.

John Knox

John Knox was a Scottish clergyman and a leader of the Protestant Reformation who brought reformation to the church in Scotland. He was educated at the University of St Andrews and was ordained to the Catholic priesthood in 1536. Influenced by early church reformers such as George Wishart, he joined the movement to reform the Scottish church. He was caught up in the ecclesiastical and political events that involved the murder of Cardinal Beaton in 1546 and the intervention of the regent of Scotland Mary of Guise.

Counter-Reformation

The Counter-Reformation was the period of Catholic revival beginning with the Council of Trent (1545-1563) and ending at the close of the Thirty Years' War (1648), which is sometimes considered a response to the Protestant Reformation. The Counter-Reformation was a comprehensive effort composed of four major elements:•Ecclesiastical or structural reconfiguration•Religious orders•Spiritual movements•Political dimensions

Such reforms included the foundation of seminaries for the proper training of priests in the spiritual life and the theological traditions of the Church, the reform of religious life by returning orders to their spiritual foundations, and new spiritual movements focusing on the devotional life and a personal relationship with Christ, including the Spanish mystics and the French school of spirituality. It also involved political activities that included the Roman Inquisition.

Stanislaus Hosius

Stanislaus Hosius was a cardinal, since 1551 Prince-Bishop in Bishopric of Warmia, Poland since 1558 papal legate to the Holy Roman Emperor's Imperial Court in Vienna, Austria and since 1566 a papal legate to Poland.

Hosius was born in Kraków as the son of Ulrich Hosse of Pforzheim and studied law at the University of Padua, Italy and the University of Bologna, Italy. He became Bishop of Chelmno in 1549 and Prince-Bishop of Warmia in 1551. Hosius had Jesuit sympathies and actively opposed the Protestant Reformation.

Visit Cram101.com for full Practice Exams

Eastern Europe

Eastern Europe is the eastern part of the European continent. The term has widely disparate and varying geopolitical, geographical, cultural and socioeconomic readings, which makes it highly context-dependent and even volatile, and there are 'almost as many definitions of Eastern Europe as there are scholars of the region'. A related United Nations paper adds that 'every assessment of spatial identities is essentially a social and cultural construct'.

Council of Trent

The Council of Trent was an Ecumenical Council of the Roman Catholic Church. It is considered to be one of the Church's most important councils. It convened in Trento, Italy, then the capital of the Prince-Bishopric of Trent of the Holy Roman Empire, between December 13, 1545, and December 4, 1563 in twenty-five sessions for three periods.

Desiderius Erasmus

Desiderius Erasmus Roterodamus (October 28, 1466 - July 12, 1536), sometimes known as Desiderius Erasmus of Rotterdam, was a Dutch Renaissance humanist and a Catholic priest and theologian. His scholarly name Desiderius Erasmus Roterodamus comprises the following three elements: the Latin noun desiderium ; the Greek adjective ?ρ?σμιος (erásmios) meaning 'desired', and, in the form Erasmus, also the name of a St. Erasmus of Formiae; and the Latinized adjectival form for the city of Rotterdam (Roterodamus = 'of Rotterdam').

Erasmus was a classical scholar who wrote in a 'pure' Latin style and enjoyed the sobriquet 'Prince of the Humanists.' He has been called 'the crowning glory of the Christian humanists.' Using humanist techniques for working on texts, he prepared important new Latin and Greek editions of the New Testament.

Inquisition

The Inquisition was a group of institutions within the judicial system of the Roman Catholic Church whose aim was to 'fight against heretics'. It started in 12th-century France to combat the spread of heresy and error, and was later expanded to other European countries, as well as throughout the Spanish and Portuguese empires in the Americas, Asia and Africa.

Historical phases of the Inquisition include: the Medieval Inquisition; the Spanish Inquisition; the Portuguese Inquisition; and the Roman Inquisition.

The term Inquisition can apply to any one of several institutions which fought against heretics within the justice system of the Roman Catholic Church.

Papal States

The Papal States were territories in the Italian peninsula under the sovereign direct rule of the Pope, from the 500s until 1870. They were among the major states of Italy from roughly the sixth century until the Italian peninsula was unified in 1861 by the Kingdom of Piedmont-Sardinia. After 1861 the Papal States, in less territorially extensive form, continued to exist until 1870. At their most extensive they covered most of the modern Italian regions of Romagna, Marche, Umbria and Lazio. This was commonly called the temporal power of the Pope, as opposed to his ecclesiastical primacy.

Visit Cram101.com for full Practice Exams

Roman Inquisition

The Roman Inquisition was a system of tribunals developed by the Holy In the period after the Medieval Inquisition, it was one of three different manifestations of the wider Christian Inquisition along with the Spanish Inquisition and Portuguese Inquisition. Objectives

Like other iterations of the Inquisition, the Roman Inquisition was responsible for prosecuting individuals accused of committing offences relating to heresy, including Protestantism, sorcery, immorality, blasphemy, Judaizing and witchcraft, as well as for censorship of printed literature.

The tribunals of the Roman Inquisition covered most of the Italian peninsula as well as Malta and also existed in isolated pockets of papal jurisdiction in other parts of Europe, including Avignon in France.

Church of Scotland

The Church of Scotland, (Scottish Gaelic: Eaglais na h-Alba, Scots: Kirk o Scotland) known informally by its Scots language name, the Kirk, is a Presbyterian church, decisively shaped by the Scottish Reformation.

The Church of Scotland traces its roots back to the beginnings of Christianity in Scotland, but its identity is principally shaped by the Reformation of 1560. Its current pledged membership is about 9% of the Scottish population--though according to the 2001 national census, 42% of the Scottish population claim some form of allegiance to it . History

While the Church of Scotland traces its roots back to the earliest Christians in Scotland, its identity was principally shaped by the Scottish Reformation of 1560. At that point, the church in Scotland broke with Rome, in a process of Protestant reform led, among others, by John Knox.

Ignatius of Loyola

St. Ignatius of Loyola was a Spanish knight from a local noble family, hermit, priest since 1537, and theologian, who founded the Society of Jesus (Jesuits) and was its first Superior General. Ignatius emerged as a religious leader during the Counter-Reformation. Loyola's devotion to the Catholic Church was characterized by absolute obedience to the Pope.

Carmelites

The Order of the Brothers of Our Lady of Mount Carmel or Carmelites is a Catholic religious order perhaps founded in the 12th century on Mount Carmel, hence its name. However, historical records about its origin remain uncertain. Saint Bertold has traditionally been associated with the founding of the order, but few clear records of early Carmelite history have survived and this is likely to be a later extrapolation by hagiographers.

Catherine de' Medici

Catherine de' Medici was born in Florence, Italy, as Caterina Maria Romula di Lorenzo de' Medici.

Both her parents, Lorenzo II de' Medici, Duke of Urbino, and Madeleine de La Tour d'Auvergne, Countess of Boulogne, died within weeks of her birth.

Concordat of Bologna

The Concordat of Bologna marking a stage in the evolution of the Gallican Church, was an agreement between King Francis I of France and Pope Leo X that Francis negotiated in the wake of his victory at Marignano in September 1515. The groundwork was laid in a series of personal meetings of king and pope in Bologna, 11-15 December 1515. The concordat was signed in Rome on 18 August 1516.

The Concordat explicitly superseded the Pragmatic Sanction of Bourges, (1438), which had proved ineffective in guaranteeing the privileges of the Church in France, where bishoprics and abbacies had been wrangled over even before the Parlement of Paris: 'hardly anywhere were elections held in due form', R. Aubenas observes, 'for the king succeeded in foisting his own candidates upon the electors by every conceivable means, not excluding the most ruthless.'

The Concordat permitted the Pope to collect all the income that the Catholic Church made in France, while the King of France was confirmed in his right to tithe the clerics and to restrict their right of appeal to Rome. The Concordat confirmed the King of France's right to nominate appointments to benefices-archbishops, bishops, abbots and priors- enabling the Crown, by controlling its personnel, to decide who was to lead the Gallican Church.

Edict of Nantes

The Edict of Nantes, issued on April 13, 1598, by Henry IV of France, granted the Calvinist Protestants of France (also known as Huguenots) substantial rights in a nation still considered essentially Catholic. In the Edict Henry aimed primarily to promote civil unity. The Edict separated civil from religious unity, treated some Protestants for the first time as more than mere schismatics and heretics, and opened a path for secularism and tolerance.

Politique

Politique rulers cared more about citizens simply obeying the laws and not of what religion they were. In the political parlance of ancien régime France, a politique was a ruler who governed without letting his or her personal feelings get in the way of doing what was best for his country.

The term was used during the sixteenth and seventeenth century Wars of Religion to describe moderates of both religious faiths (Huguenots and Catholics) who held that only the restoration of a strong monarchy could save France from total collapse.

Union of Utrecht

The Union of Utrecht is a federation of Old Catholic Churches, not in communion with Rome, that seceded from the Roman Catholic Church over the issue of Papal infallibility. The Declaration of Utrecht solidified this movement in 1889. The Union of Utrecht is in full communion with the Anglican Communion, as per the Bonn Agreement of 1931, and with the Philippine Independent Church.

The Old Catholic Churches reject the doctrine of papal infallibility; thus they reject the dogmatic status of the teachings promulgated in the Roman Catholic Church by such means, namely the Immaculate Conception and Assumption of Mary.

14. Reformations and Religious Wars, 1500-1600

CHAPTER HIGHLIGHTS & NOTES: KEY TERMS, PEOPLE, PLACES, CONCEPTS

Abdication	Abdication occurs when a monarch, such as a king or emperor, renounces her or his office. meaning to disown or renounce (from ab, away from, and dicare, to declare, to proclaim as not belonging to one). In its broadest sense abdication is the act of renouncing and resigning from any formal office, but especially from the supreme office of state.
Religious persecution	Religious persecution is the systematic mistreatment of an individual or group of individuals as a response to their religious beliefs or affiliations or lack thereof. The tendency of societies or groups within society to alienate or repress different subcultures is a recurrent theme in human history. Moreover, because a person's religion often determines to a significant extent his or her morality and personal identity, religious differences can be significant cultural factors.

CHAPTER QUIZ: KEY TERMS, PEOPLE, PLACES, CONCEPTS

1. The _________ was a varying complex of lands that existed from 962 to 1806 in Central Europe. It grew out of East Francia, one of the primary divisions of the Frankish Empire. Its character changed during the Middle Ages and the Early Modern period, when the power of the emperor gradually weakened in favour of the princes.

    a. Huis Doorn
    b. Hungarians in Germany
    c. Johanna Sibylla of Hanau-Lichtenberg
    d. Holy Roman Empire

2. The _________, issued on April 13, 1598, by Henry IV of France, granted the Calvinist Protestants of France (also known as Huguenots) substantial rights in a nation still considered essentially Catholic. In the Edict Henry aimed primarily to promote civil unity. The Edict separated civil from religious unity, treated some Protestants for the first time as more than mere schismatics and heretics, and opened a path for secularism and tolerance.

    a. Edict of Versailles
    b. Edict on Idle Institutions
    c. Edict of Nantes
    d. Papal conclave, 1523

3. . The _________, is a list of religious and moral imperatives that, according to the Hebrew Bible, were given by God to the people of Israel from the mountain referred to as Mount Sinai or Horeb. The Bible describes their form as being spoken by God and subsequently as an inscription on two stone tablets which God wrote with his finger, after which God gave the tablets to Moses. The _________ are recognized as a moral foundation in Judaism and Christianity.

Visit Cram101.com for full Practice Exams

a. Erik the Red
b. D. P. Moran
c. Ten Commandments
d. Julia Antonia

4. In the Catholic Church, a _________ is an ordained minister who holds the fullness of the sacrament of Holy Orders and is responsible for teaching doctrine, governing Catholics in his jurisdiction, and sanctifying the world and for representing the Church. Catholics trace the origins of the office of _________ to the apostles, who were endowed with a special charism by the Holy Spirit at Pentecost. Catholics believe this special charism has been transmitted through an unbroken succession of _________s by the laying on of hands in the sacrament of Holy Orders.

a. Bulacan Philippines Annual Conference
b. Cafe church
c. Cell church
d. Bishop

5. The branch of Christian theology that deals with _________ and redemption is called Soteriology. It is derived from Greek soterion (_________) (from soter 'savior, redeemer') + English -logy.

Speaking only within the scope of Christian theology in this article, soteriology examines the role of Jesus Christ as saviour, and redeemer.

a. Christian tradition
b. Christian Universalism
c. Salvation
d. Christian worship

Visit Cram101.com for full Practice Exams

ANSWER KEY
14. Reformations and Religious Wars, 1500-1600

1. d
2. c
3. c
4. d
5. c

You can take the complete Chapter Practice Test

for 14. Reformations and Religious Wars, 1500-1600
on all key terms, persons, places, and concepts.

Online 99 Cents

http://www.epub141.56.21995.14.cram101.com/

Use www.Cram101.com for all your study needs

including Cram101's online interactive problem solving labs in

chemistry, statistics, mathematics, and more.

15. European Exploration and Conquest, 1450-1650

CHAPTER OUTLINE: KEY TERMS, PEOPLE, PLACES, CONCEPTS

_____ Age of Discovery

_____ Dutch East India Company

_____ Java

_____ Conquistador

_____ Caravel

_____ John Mandeville

_____ Christopher Columbus

_____ Prester John

_____ Treaty of Tordesillas

_____ The Bowman and The Spearman

_____ John Cabot

_____ Tenochtitlan

_____ Inca Empire

_____ Mexica

_____ Atlantic

_____ Catholic Church

_____ Plymouth Colony

_____ Providence

_____ Seven Years' War

_____ Tobacco

_____ Hacienda

15. European Exploration and Conquest, 1450-1650

CHAPTER OUTLINE: KEY TERMS, PEOPLE, PLACES, CONCEPTS

- New Spain
- Hispanic America
- European colonization of the Americas
- Columbian Exchange
- Canary Islands
- East India Company
- Cultural relativism
- William Shakespeare

CHAPTER HIGHLIGHTS & NOTES: KEY TERMS, PEOPLE, PLACES, CONCEPTS

Age of Discovery	The Age of Discovery, was a period starting in the early 15th century and continuing to the 17th century during which Europeans explored Africa, the Americas, Asia and Oceania. The fall of Constantinople in 1453 severed European trade links by land with Asia leading many to begin seeking routes east by sea and spurred the age of exploration. Historians often refer to the 'Age of Discovery' as the pioneer Portuguese and Spanish long-distance maritime travels in search of alternative trade routes to 'the East Indies', moved by the trade of gold, silver and spices.
Dutch East India Company	The Dutch East India Company was a chartered company established in 1602, when the States-General of the Netherlands granted it a 21-year monopoly to carry out colonial activities in Asia. It is often considered to have been the first multinational corporation in the world and it was the first company to issue stock. It was also arguably the first megacorporation, possessing quasi-governmental powers, including the ability to wage war, imprison and execute convicts, negotiate treaties, coin money, and establish colonies.
Java	Java is a dance which was developed in France in the early part of the 20th century. The origin of its name is uncertain, but it probably evolved from the mazurka.

15. European Exploration and Conquest, 1450-1650

CHAPTER HIGHLIGHTS & NOTES: KEY TERMS, PEOPLE, PLACES, CONCEPTS

Conquistador	Conquistador is the term widely used to refer to the Spanish and Portuguese soldiers, explorers, and adventurers who brought much of the Americas under the control of Spain and Portugal in the 15th to 19th centuries following Europe's discovery of the New World by Christopher Columbus in 1492. The two perhaps most famous conquistadores were Hernán Cortés who conquered the Aztec Empire and Francisco Pizarro who led the conquest of the Incan Empire. The conquistadors in the Americas were more volunteer militia than an actual organized military. They had to supply their own materials, weapons and horses.
Caravel	A caravel is a small, highly maneuverable sailing ship developed in the 15th century by the Portuguese to explore along the West African coast and into the Atlantic Ocean. The lateen sails gave her speed and the capacity for sailing to windward (beating). Caravels were much used by the Portuguese for the oceanic exploration voyages during the 15th and 16th centuries in the age of discovery.
John Mandeville	'Jehan de Mandeville', translated as 'Sir John Mandeville', is the name claimed by the compiler of The Travels of Sir John Mandeville, a book account of his supposed travels, written in Anglo-Norman French, and first circulated between 1357 and 1371. By aid of translations into many other languages it acquired extraordinary popularity. Despite the extremely unreliable and often fantastical nature of the travels it describes, it was used as a work of reference -- Christopher Columbus, for example, was heavily influenced by both this work and Marco Polo's earlier Il Milione (Adams 53).
Christopher Columbus	Christopher Columbus was an explorer, navigator, and colonizer, born in the Republic of Genoa, in what is today northwestern Italy. Under the auspices of the Catholic Monarchs of Spain, he completed four voyages across the Atlantic Ocean that led to general European awareness of the American continents. Those voyages, and his efforts to establish permanent settlements on the island of Hispaniola, initiated the Spanish colonization of the New World.
Prester John	The legends of Prester John were popular in Europe from the 12th through the 17th centuries, and told of a Christian patriarch and king said to rule over a Christian nation lost amidst the Muslims and pagans in the Orient. Written accounts of this kingdom are variegated collections of medieval popular fantasy. Prester John was reportedly a descendant of one of the Three Magi, said to be a generous ruler and a virtuous man, presiding over a realm full of riches and strange creatures, in which the Patriarch of the Saint Thomas Christians resided.
Treaty of Tordesillas	The Treaty of Tordesillas, signed at Tordesillas (now in Valladolid province, Spain) on 7 June 1494, divided the newly discovered lands outside Europe between Portugal and Spain along a meridian 370 leagues west of the Cape Verde islands (off the west coast of Africa).

This line of demarcation was about halfway between the Cape Verde Islands and the islands discovered by Christopher Columbus on his first voyage (claimed for Spain), named in the treaty as Cipangu and Antilia (Cuba and Hispaniola).

The lands to the east would belong to Portugal and the lands to the west to Spain.

The Bowman and The Spearman

The Bowman and The Spearman, are two bronze equestrian sculptures standing as gatekeepers at the intersection of Congress Drive and Michigan Avenue in Grant Park, Chicago, United States. The sculptures were made in Zagreb by Croatian sculptor Ivan Meštrovic and installed at the entrance of the parkway in 1928. The pair of sculptures was funded by the Benjamin Ferguson Fund.

An unusual aspect of the sculptures is that the figures in both sculptures are missing their weapons, the bow and arrow and the spear.

John Cabot

John Cabot was an Italian navigator and explorer whose 1497 discovery of parts of North America under the commission of Henry VII of England is commonly held to have been the first European encounter with the continent of North America since the Norse Vikings in the eleventh century. The official position of the Canadian and United Kingdom governments is that he landed on the island of Newfoundland.

Cabot's birthplace is in Italy.

Tenochtitlan

Tenochtitlan was a Nahua altepetl (city-state) located on an island in Lake Texcoco, in the Valley of Mexico. Founded in 1325, it became the capital of the abounding Aztec Empire in the 15th century, until captured by the Spanish in 1521. When paired with Mexico the name is a reference to Mexica, the people of the surrounding Aztec heartland. It subsequently became a cabecera of the Viceroyalty of New Spain, and today the ruins of Tenochtitlan are located in the central part of Mexico City.

Inca Empire

The Inca Empire, was the largest empire in pre-Columbian America. The administrative, political and military center of the empire was located in Cusco in modern-day Peru. The Inca civilization arose from the highlands of Peru sometime in the early 13th century.

From 1438 to 1533, the Incas used a variety of methods, from conquest to peaceful assimilation, to incorporate a large portion of western South America, centered on the Andean mountain ranges, including, besides Peru, large parts of modern Ecuador, western and south central Bolivia, northwest Argentina, north and central Chile, and southern Colombia into a state comparable to the historical empires of Eurasia.

15. European Exploration and Conquest, 1450-1650

Mexica

The Mexica or Mexicas - called Aztecs in occidental historiography, although this term is not limited to the Mexica - were an indigenous people of the Valley of Mexico, known today as the rulers of the Aztec empire. The Mexica were a Nahua people who founded their two cities Tenochtitlan and Tlatelolco on raised islets in Lake Texcoco around AD 1200. After the rise of the Tenochca Mexica they came to dominate the other Mexica city-state Tlatelolco.

The Mexica are eponymous of the placename Mexico Mexihco [me?'?i?ko].

Atlantic

The Atlantic in palaeoclimatology was the warmest and moistest Blytt-Sernander period, pollen zone and chronozone of Holocene northern Europe. The climate was generally warmer than today. It was preceded by the Boreal, with a climate similar to today's, and was followed by the Subboreal, a transition to the modern.

Catholic Church

The Catholic Church, is the world's largest Christian church. Headed by the Pope, it sees its mission as spreading the gospel of Christ, administering its sacraments and exercising charity.

The Catholic Church is one of the oldest religious institutions in the world and has played a prominent role in the history of Western civilisation.

Plymouth Colony

Plymouth Colony was an English colonial venture in North America from 1620 to 1691. The first settlement of the Plymouth Colony was at New Plymouth, a location previously surveyed and named by Captain John Smith. The settlement, which served as the capital of the colony, is today the modern town of Plymouth, Massachusetts. At its height, Plymouth Colony occupied most of the southeastern portion of the modern state of Massachusetts.

Providence

Providence is a Christian religious movement most notable for its bible study formerly called the 30 lessons, for the controversies surrounding its founder, and its fast growth. From the time it was founded 30 years ago in Korea, Providence churches have been established in 50 nations including United States, England, France, Germany, Japan, Taiwan, Korea, Canada, Malaysia, Singapore, Australia, and New Zealand. The movement was originally founded in South Korea which is still where it has the most members.

Seven Years' War

The Seven Years' War was a global military conflict between 1756 and 1763, involving most of the great powers of the time affecting North and Central America, Europe, the West African coast, India and the Philippines. espective theaters: French and Indian War (North America, 1754-1763), Pomeranian War (Sweden, 1757-1762), Third Carnatic War (India, 1757-1763) and Third Silesian War .

Visit Cram101.com for full Practice Exams

Tobacco	Tobacco is a product processed from the dried leaves of plants in the genus Nicotiana. It can be used as a pesticide, and extracts form ingredients of some medicines, but is most commonly consumed as a drug. Tobacco is a name for any plant of the genus Nicotiana of the Solanaceae family (nightshade family) and for the product manufactured from the leaf used in cigars and cigarettes, snuff, pipe tobacco, chewing tobacco, and flavored shisha.
Hacienda	Hacienda is a Spanish word for an estate. Some haciendas were plantations, mines, or even business factories. Many haciendas combined these productive activities.
New Spain	New Spain, formally called the Viceroyalty of New Spain, was a viceroyalty of the crown of Castile, of the Spanish empire, comprising territories in the north overseas 'Septentrion' (North America and Philippines). New Spain was established following the Spanish conquest of the Aztec Empire in 1521. Its greatest extent included much of North America south of Canada, that is: all of present-day Mexico and Central America except Panama; most of the United States west of the Mississippi River, plus the Floridas. New Spain also included: the Spanish East Indies (the Philippine Islands, the Mariana Islands, the Caroline Islands, Taiwan, and parts of the Moluccas); and the Spanish West Indies (Cuba, Hispaniola (comprising Haiti and the Dominican Republic), Puerto Rico, Jamaica, the Cayman Islands, Trinidad, and the Bay Islands).
Hispanic America	Hispanic America is the region comprising the American countries inhabited by Spanish-speaking populations. These countries have significant commonalities with each other and with Spain, whose colonies they formerly were. In all of these countries, Spanish is the main language, sometimes sharing official status with one or more indigenous languages, or English (in Puerto Rico).
European colonization of the Americas	The start of the European colonization of the Americas is typically dated to 1492, although there was at least one earlier colonization effort.The first known Europeans to reach the Americas were the Vikings (Norse) during the 11th century, who established several colonies in Greenland and one short-lived settlement at L'Anse aux Meadows (51°N) in the area the Norse called Vinland, present day Newfoundland and to the south. Settlements in Greenland survived for several centuries, during which time the Greenland Norse and the Inuit people experienced mostly hostile contact. By the end of the 15th century, the Norse Greenland settlements had collapsed.
Columbian Exchange	The Columbian Exchange, was a dramatically widespread exchange of animals, plants, culture, human populations (including slaves), communicable disease, and ideas between the American and Afro-Eurasian hemispheres following the voyage to the Americas by Christopher Columbus in 1492. The term was coined in 1972 by Alfred W. Crosby, a historian at the University of Texas at Austin, in his eponymous work of environmental history.

The contact between the two areas circulated a wide variety of new crops and livestock which supported increases in population in both hemispheres. Explorers returned to Europe with maize, potatoes, and tomatoes, which became very important crops in Europe by the 18th century.

Canary Islands

The Canary Islands are a Spanish archipelago located just off the northwest coast of mainland Africa, 100 km west of the border between Morocco and the Western Sahara. The Canaries are a Spanish autonomous community and an outermost region of the European Union. The islands include (from largest to smallest): Tenerife, Fuerteventura, Gran Canaria, Lanzarote, La Palma, La Gomera, El Hierro, and the islets La Graciosa, Alegranza, Montaña Clara, Roque del Este, Roque del Oeste and Isla de Lobos.

East India Company

The East India Company originally chartered as the Governor and Company of Merchants of London trading into the East Indies, and often called the Honourable East India Company, was an English and later (from 1707) British joint-stock company and megacorporation formed for pursuing trade with the East Indies but which ended up trading mainly with the Indian subcontinent, North-west frontier province and Balochistan.

The East India Company traded mainly in cotton, silk, indigo dye, salt, saltpetre, tea and opium. The Company was granted a Royal Charter by Queen Elizabeth in 1600, making it the oldest among several similarly formed European East India Companies.

Cultural relativism

Cultural relativism is the principle that an individual human's beliefs and activities should be understood by others in terms of that individual's own culture. This principle was established as axiomatic in anthropological research by Franz Boas in the first few decades of the 20th century and later popularized by his students. Boas first articulated the idea in 1887: '...civilization is not something absolute, but ... is relative, and ... our ideas and conceptions are true only so far as our civilization goes.' but did not actually coin the term 'cultural relativism.'

The first use of the term recorded in the Oxford English Dictionary was by philosopher and social theorist Alain Locke in 1924 to describe Robert Lowie's 'extreme cultural relativism', found in the latter's 1917 book Culture and Ethnology.

William Shakespeare

William Shakespeare (26 April 1564 (baptised) - 23 April 1616) was an English poet and playwright, widely regarded as the greatest writer in the English language and the world's pre-eminent dramatist. He is often called England's national poet and the 'Bard of Avon'. His extant works, including some collaborations, consist of about 38 plays, 154 sonnets, two long narrative poems, two epitaphs on a man named John Combe, one epitaph on Elias James, and several other poems.

Visit Cram101.com for full Practice Exams

1. 'Jehan de Mandeville', translated as 'Sir _________', is the name claimed by the compiler of The Travels of Sir _________, a book account of his supposed travels, written in Anglo-Norman French, and first circulated between 1357 and 1371.

   By aid of translations into many other languages it acquired extraordinary popularity. Despite the extremely unreliable and often fantastical nature of the travels it describes, it was used as a work of reference -- Christopher Columbus, for example, was heavily influenced by both this work and Marco Polo's earlier Il Milione (Adams 53).

   a. Mare
   b. John Mandeville
   c. Matter of England
   d. John Middleton

2. The _________, was a period starting in the early 15th century and continuing to the 17th century during which Europeans explored Africa, the Americas, Asia and Oceania. The fall of Constantinople in 1453 severed European trade links by land with Asia leading many to begin seeking routes east by sea and spurred the age of exploration. Historians often refer to the '_________' as the pioneer Portuguese and Spanish long-distance maritime travels in search of alternative trade routes to 'the East Indies', moved by the trade of gold, silver and spices.

   a. Axial Age
   b. Edwardian era
   c. Age of Discovery
   d. Information Age

3. The _________, signed at Tordesillas (now in Valladolid province, Spain) on 7 June 1494, divided the newly discovered lands outside Europe between Portugal and Spain along a meridian 370 leagues west of the Cape Verde islands (off the west coast of Africa). This line of demarcation was about halfway between the Cape Verde Islands and the islands discovered by Christopher Columbus on his first voyage (claimed for Spain), named in the treaty as Cipangu and Antilia (Cuba and Hispaniola).

   The lands to the east would belong to Portugal and the lands to the west to Spain.

   a. Diego de Vargas
   b. Second Servile War
   c. Treaty of Tordesillas
   d. Battle of Guinea

4. . _________ was an explorer, navigator, and colonizer, born in the Republic of Genoa, in what is today northwestern Italy. Under the auspices of the Catholic Monarchs of Spain, he completed four voyages across the Atlantic Ocean that led to general European awareness of the American continents. Those voyages, and his efforts to establish permanent settlements on the island of Hispaniola, initiated the Spanish colonization of the New World.

   a. Erik the Red
   b. Matter of Britain

c. Christopher Columbus
d. John Middleton

5. The _________ or _________s - called Aztecs in occidental historiography, although this term is not limited to the _________ - were an indigenous people of the Valley of Mexico, known today as the rulers of the Aztec empire. The _________ were a Nahua people who founded their two cities Tenochtitlan and Tlatelolco on raised islets in Lake Texcoco around AD 1200. After the rise of the Tenochca _________ they came to dominate the other _________ city-state Tlatelolco.

   The _________ are eponymous of the placename Mexico Mexihco [me?'?i?ko].

   a. Yaocihuatl
   b. Mexica
   c. Second Servile War
   d. Dimasaua

Visit Cram101.com for full Practice Exams

ANSWER KEY
15. European Exploration and Conquest, 1450-1650

1. b
2. c
3. c
4. c
5. b

You can take the complete Chapter Practice Test

for 15. European Exploration and Conquest, 1450-1650
on all key terms, persons, places, and concepts.

Online 99 Cents

http://www.epub141.56.21995.15.cram101.com/

Use www.Cram101.com for all your study needs

including Cram101's online interactive problem solving labs in

chemistry, statistics, mathematics, and more.

16. Absolutism and Constitutionalism in Europe, ca. 1589-1725

CHAPTER OUTLINE: KEY TERMS, PEOPLE, PLACES, CONCEPTS

Food riot

Little Ice Age

Eastern Europe

Peace of Augsburg

Thirty Years' War

French and Indian War

Peace of Westphalia

Popular Action

Catholic Church

Edict of Nantes

Fronde

Protestantism

Louis Jolliet

Minorca

War of the Spanish Succession

Asiento

Bohemian

Transylvania

Treaty of the Pyrenees

Independence of Brazil

Prussia

16. Absolutism and Constitutionalism in Europe, ca. 1589-1725

CHAPTER OUTLINE: KEY TERMS, PEOPLE, PLACES, CONCEPTS

______ Baltic region

______ Boyar

______ Orthodox Christianity

______ Absolutism

______ Society

______ Great Northern War

______ Harem

______ Divine right of kings

______ House of Commons

______ Peter Paul Rubens

______ Puritan

______ William Laud

______ Catholicism

______ New Model Army

______ Rump Parliament

______ Navigation Acts

______ David Hume

______ John Locke

______ Heinrich Heine

______ Dutch Republic

______ Golden Age

Visit Cram101.com for full Practice Exams

Food riot

Food riots occur if there is shortage of food and/or unequal distribution of food. Causes can be harvest failures, incompetent food storage, transport problems, food speculation, hoarding, poisoning of food, or attacks by pests like locusts. When the public becomes too desperate in such conditions, they may attack shops, farms, homes, or government buildings to attain bread or other staple foods like grain or salt, as in the 1977 Egyptian Bread Riots .

Little Ice Age

The Little Ice Age was a period of cooling that occurred after the Medieval Warm Period (Medieval Climate Optimum). While it was not a true ice age, the term was introduced into the scientific literature by François E. Matthes in 1939. It has been conventionally defined as a period extending from the 16th to the 19th centuries, or alternatively, from about 1350 to about 1850, though climatologists and historians working with local records no longer expect to agree on either the start or end dates of this period, which varied according to local conditions. NASA defines the term as a cold period between AD 1550 and AD 1850 and notes three particularly cold intervals: one beginning about 1650, another about 1770, and the last in 1850, each separated by intervals of slight warming.

Eastern Europe

Eastern Europe is the eastern part of the European continent. The term has widely disparate and varying geopolitical, geographical, cultural and socioeconomic readings, which makes it highly context-dependent and even volatile, and there are 'almost as many definitions of Eastern Europe as there are scholars of the region'. A related United Nations paper adds that 'every assessment of spatial identities is essentially a social and cultural construct'.

Peace of Augsburg

The Peace of Augsburg, was a treaty between Charles V and the forces of the Schmalkaldic League, an alliance of Lutheran princes, on September 25, 1555, at the imperial city of Augsburg, now in present-day Bavaria, Germany.

It officially ended the religious struggle between the two groups and made the legal division of Christendom permanent within the Holy Roman Empire. The Peace established the principle Cuius regio, eius religio, which allowed Holy Roman Empire's states' princes to select either Lutheranism or Catholicism within the domains they controlled, ultimately reaffirming the independence they had over their states.

Thirty Years' War

The Thirty Years' War was a series of wars principally fought in Central Europe, involving most of the countries of Europe. It was one of the longest and most destructive conflicts in European history, and one of the longest continuous wars in modern history.

The origins of the conflict and goals of the participants were complex and no single cause can accurately be described as the main reason for the fighting. Initially, it was fought largely as a religious war between Protestants and Catholics in the Holy Roman Empire, although disputes over internal politics and the balance of power within the Empire played a significant part. Gradually, it developed into a more general conflict involving most of the great powers of the time.

16. Absolutism and Constitutionalism in Europe, ca. 1589-1725

CHAPTER HIGHLIGHTS & NOTES: KEY TERMS, PEOPLE, PLACES, CONCEPTS

French and Indian War

The French and Indian War is the name for the North American theater of the Seven Years War. The war was fought primarily between the colonies of Great Britain and New France, with both sides supported by military troops from Europe. In 1756, the war erupted into the world-wide conflict involving Britain and France.

Peace of Westphalia

The Peace of Westphalia was a series of peace treaties signed between May and October 1648 in Osnabrück and Münster. These treaties ended the Thirty Years' War (1618-1648) in the Holy Roman Empire, and the Eighty Years' War (1568-1648) between Spain and the Dutch Republic, with Spain formally recognizing the independence of the Dutch Republic.

The Peace of Westphalia treaties involved the Holy Roman Emperor, Ferdinand III, of the House of Habsburg, the Kingdom of Spain, the Kingdom of France, the Swedish Empire, the Dutch Republic, the Princes of the Holy Roman Empire, and sovereigns of the free imperial cities and can be denoted by two major events:•The signing of the Peace of Münster between the Dutch Republic and the Kingdom of Spain on 30 January 1648, officially ratified in Münster on 15 May 1648•The signing of two complementary treaties on 24 October 1648, namely:•The Treaty of Münster (Instrumentum Pacis Monasteriensis, IPM), concerning the Holy Roman Emperor and France and their respective allies•The Treaty of Osnabrück (Instrumentum Pacis Osnabrugensis, IPO), concerning the Holy Roman Emperor, the Empire and Sweden and their respective allies

The treaties resulted from the big diplomatic congress, thereby initiating a new system of political order in central Europe, later called Westphalian sovereignty, based upon the concept of a sovereign state governed by a sovereign and establishing a prejudice in international affairs against interference in another nation's domestic business.

Popular Action

Popular Action is a centrist and social liberal party in Peru.

Fernando Belaúnde founded Popular Action in 1956 as a reformist alternative to the status quo conservative forces and the controversial American Popular Revolutionary Alliance party.

Although Belaúnde's message was not all that different from APRA's, his tactics were more inclusive and less confrontational.

Catholic Church

The Catholic Church, is the world's largest Christian church. Headed by the Pope, it sees its mission as spreading the gospel of Christ, administering its sacraments and exercising charity.

The Catholic Church is one of the oldest religious institutions in the world and has played a prominent role in the history of Western civilisation.

Edict of Nantes

The Edict of Nantes, issued on April 13, 1598, by Henry IV of France, granted the Calvinist Protestants of France (also known as Huguenots) substantial rights in a nation still considered essentially Catholic. In the Edict Henry aimed primarily to promote civil unity.

Fronde

The Fronde was a civil war in France, occurring in the midst of the Franco-Spanish War, which had begun in 1635. The word fronde means sling, which Parisian mobs used to smash the windows of supporters of Cardinal Mazarin.

The Fronde was divided into two campaigns, the Fronde of the parlements and the Fronde of the nobles. The timing of the outbreak of the Fronde des parlements, directly after the Peace of Westphalia (1648) that ended the Thirty Years War, was significant.

Protestantism

Protestantism is one of the major groupings within Christianity. It has been defined as 'any of several church denominations denying the universal authority of the Pope and affirming the Reformation principles of justification by faith alone, the priesthood of all believers, and the primacy of the Bible as the only source of revealed truth' and, more broadly, to mean Christianity outside 'of a Catholic or Eastern church'. It is a movement that began in Germany in the early 16th century as a reaction against medieval Roman Catholic doctrines and practices, especially in regards to salvation, justification, and ecclesiology.

Louis Jolliet

Louis Jolliet was a French Canadian explorer known for his discoveries in North America. Jolliet and Jesuit Father Jacques Marquette, a Catholic priest and missionary, were the first Europeans to explore and map much of the Mississippi River in 1673.

Minorca

The Minorca is a breed of chicken originating in Spain. They are classified in the Mediterranean class by the American Poultry Association. They lay white eggs.

War of the Spanish Succession

The War of the Spanish Succession was fought between two alliances of European powers, including a divided Spain, over who had the right to succeed Charles II as king of Spain.

Spain suffered a steep decline in the second half of the 17th century under the reign of its last Habsburg king Charles II, so that by 1700 its neglected forces were barely considered those of a first rate power. However, it still possessed an immense territorial domain, including Milan and southern Italy, the southern Netherlands, the Philippines, vast territories in the Americas, and various other smaller territories and islands, making it by far the largest European empire.

Asiento

The Asiento in the history of slavery refers to the permission given by the Spanish government to other countries to sell people as slaves to the Spanish colonies, between the years 1543 and 1834.

In British history, it usually refers to the contract between Spain and Great Britain created in 1713 that dealt with the supply of African slaves for the Spanish territories in the Americas. The British government passed its rights to the South Sea Company.

Bohemian

A Bohemian is a resident of the former Kingdom of Bohemia, either in a narrow sense as the region of Bohemia proper or in a wider meaning as the whole country, now known as the Czech Republic.

Visit Cram101.com for full Practice Exams

The word 'Bohemian' used to denote the Czech people as well as the Czech language before the word 'Czech' became prevalent in English. The word 'Bohemian' was never used by the local Czech (Slavic) population.

Transylvania

Transylvania is a 2006 French drama film starring Asia Argento. In 2006, Director Tony Gatlif and composer Delphine Mantoulet won the 'Georges Delerue Prize' at the Flanders International Film Festival for the score, and Gatlif was nominated for the 'Grand Prix' award. Transylvania premiered at the 2006 Cannes Film Festival in France on May 28, and premiered at in the United States on March 16, 2007 at the Cleveland International Film Festival and in the United Kingdom at the Cambridge Film Festival on July 6, 2007 (with a later theatrical release on August 10, 2007).

Treaty of the Pyrenees

The Treaty of the Pyrenees was signed to end the 1635 to 1659 war between France and Spain, a war that was initially a part of the wider Thirty Years' War. It was signed on Pheasant Island, a river island on the border between the two countries. The kings Louis XIV of France and Philip IV of Spain were represented by their chief ministers, Cardinal Mazarin and Don Luis de Haro, respectively.

Independence of Brazil

The Independence of Brazil comprised a series of political events that occurred in 1821-1824, most of which involved disputes between Brazil and Portugal regarding the call for independence presented by the Brazilian Empire. It is celebrated on September 7. Background Origin of Brazil

The land now called Brazil was claimed by Portugal in April 1500, on the arrival of the Portuguese fleet commanded by Pedro Álvares Cabral.

Prussia

Prussia is a historical region in Central Europe extending from the south-eastern coast of the Baltic Sea to the Masurian Lake District. It is now divided between Poland, Russia, and Lithuania. The former German state of Prussia derived its name from the region.

Baltic region

The terms Baltic region, Baltic Rim countries, and Baltic Rim refer to slightly different combinations of countries in the general area surrounding the Baltic Sea.

Etymology

The first to name it the Baltic Sea ('Mare Balticum') was eleventh century German chronicler Adam of Bremen.

Denotation

Depending on the context the Baltic region might stand for:•The countries that have shorelines along the Baltic Sea: Denmark, Estonia, Latvia, Finland, Germany, Lithuania, Poland, Russia, and Sweden.•The group of countries presently referred to by the short-hand Baltic states: Estonia, Latvia, and Lithuania, sometimes in addition the Russian Kaliningrad exclave.•Historic East Prussia and the historical lands of Livonia, Courland and Estonia .•The former Baltic province of Imperial Russia: Today's Estonia, Latvia, Lithuania .•The countries on the historical British trade route through the Baltic Sea, i.e. including the Scandinavian Peninsula (Sweden and Norway).•The Council of the Baltic Sea States, comprised by the countries with shorelines along the Baltic Sea, in addition to Norway, Iceland and the rest of European Union.•The islands of the Euroregion B7 Baltic Seven Islands, which includes the islands and archipelagos Åland (autonomous), Bornholm (Denmark), Gotland (Sweden), Hiiumaa (Estonia), Öland (Sweden), Rügen, and Saaremaa (Estonia).•On historic Scandinavian and German maps, the Balticum sometimes includes only the historically or culturally German-dominated lands, or provinces, of Estonia, Livonia, Courland and Latgale (corresponding to modern Estonia and Latvia), as well as sometimes Pommerania and East Prussia, while the historically less-Germanized Lithuania is occasionally excluded..

Boyar

A boyar, Kievan Rus'ian, Bulgarian, Wallachian, and Moldavian aristocracies, second only to the ruling princes (in Bulgaria, tsars), from the 10th century through the 17th century. The rank has lived on as a surname in Russia and Finland, where it is spelled 'Pajari'.

Etymology

According to most sources the word is of Proto-Bulgarian origin.

Orthodox Christianity

The term Orthodox Christianity may refer to•Eastern Orthodoxy: the Ancient communion of Eastern Christian Churches, historically of eastern Europe and parts of Asia, that recognize the Council of Chalcedon and the other of the first seven Ecumenical Councils.•Oriental Orthodoxy: the Miaphysite Eastern Christian churches adhering to the first three Ecumenical Councils and the 449 Council of Ephesus, and rejecting the Council of Chalcedon and the later councils that Eastern Orthodoxy classifies as ecumenical.

Absolutism

Absolutism or The Age of Absolutism is a historiographical term used to describe a form of monarchical power that is unrestrained by all other institutions, such as churches, legislatures, or social elites. Absolutism is typically used in conjunction with some European monarchs during the transition from feudalism to capitalism, and monarchs described as absolute can especially be found in the 16th century through the 19th century. Absolutism is characterized by the ending of feudal partitioning, consolidation of power with the monarch, rise of state power, unification of the state laws, and a decrease in the influence of the Church and the nobility.

Society	A society, is a group of people related to each other through persistent relations, or a large social grouping sharing the same geographical or virtual territory, subject to the same political authority and dominant cultural expectations. Human societies are characterized by patterns of relationships (social relations) between individuals who share a distinctive culture and institutions; a given society may be described as the sum total of such relationships among its constituent members. In the social sciences, a larger society often evinces stratification and/or dominance patterns in subgroups.
Great Northern War	The Great Northern War was a conflict in which a coalition led by the Tsardom of Russia successfully contested the supremacy of the Swedish Empire in Northern Europe, Central Europe and Eastern Europe. The initial leaders of the anti-Swedish alliance were Peter the Great of Russia, Frederick IV of Denmark-Norway and Augustus II the Strong of Saxony-Poland-Lithuania. Frederick IV and August II were forced out of the alliance in 1700 and 1706 respectively, but re-joined it in 1709. George I of Brunswick-Lüneburg (Hanover) joined the coalition in 1714 for Hanover and in 1717 for Britain, and Frederick William I of Brandenburg-Prussia joined it in 1715.
Harem	Harem refers to the sphere of women in what is usually a polygynous household and their enclosed quarters which are forbidden to men. It originated in the Near East and is typically associated in the Western world with the Ottoman Empire. Etymology The word has been recorded in the English language since 1634, via Turkish harem, from Arabic ?aram 'forbidden', originally implying 'women's quarters', literally 'something forbidden or kept safe', from the root of ?arama 'to be forbidden; to exclude'.
Divine right of kings	The divine right of kings, is a political and religious doctrine of royal and political legitimacy. It asserts that a monarch is subject to no earthly authority, deriving his right to rule directly from the will of God. The king is thus not subject to the will of his people, the aristocracy, or any other estate of the realm, including (in the view of some, especially in Protestant countries) the Church.
House of Commons	The House of Commons was the lower house of the National Assembly of the Republic of Korea during its Second Republic. The House of Commons was established by the Constitution of the Second Republic of Korea, which established a bicameral legislature.
Peter Paul Rubens	Sir Peter Paul Rubens (Dutch pronunciation: ['ryb?(n)s]; 28 June 1577 - 30 May 1640), was a Flemish Baroque painter, and a proponent of an extravagant Baroque style that emphasised movement, colour, and sensuality. He is well known for his Counter-Reformation altarpieces, portraits, landscapes, and history paintings of mythological and allegorical subjects.

Puritan

The Puritans were a significant grouping of English Protestants in the 16th and 17th centuries, including, but not limited to, English Calvinists. Puritanism in this sense was founded by some Marian exiles from the clergy shortly after the accession of Elizabeth I of England in 1558, as an activist movement within the Church of England. The designation 'Puritan' is often incorrectly used, notably based on the assumption that hedonism and puritanism are antonyms.

William Laud

William Laud was Archbishop of Canterbury from 1633 to 1645. One of the High Church Caroline divines, he opposed radical forms of Puritanism. This, and his support for King Charles I, resulted in his beheading in the midst of the English Civil War. Clergyman

William Laud was born in a house on Broad Street in Reading, of comparatively lowly origins; his father, also named William, was a cloth merchant (a fact about which Laud was to remain sensitive throughout his career).

Catholicism

Catholicism is a broad term for the body of the Catholic faith, its theologies and doctrines, its liturgical, ethical, spiritual, and behavioral characteristics, as well as a religious people as a whole.

For many the term usually refers to Christians and churches belonging to the Roman Catholic Church in full communion with the Holy See. For others it refers to the churches of the first millennium, including, besides the Roman Catholic Church, the Eastern Orthodox Church, the Oriental Orthodox Church, and the Assyrian Church of the East.

New Model Army

The New Model Army of England was formed in 1645 by the Parliamentarians in the English Civil War, and was disbanded in 1660 after the Restoration. It differed from other armies in the series of civil wars referred to as the Wars of the Three Kingdoms in that it was intended as an army liable for service anywhere in the country (including in Scotland and Ireland), rather than being tied to a single area or garrison. Its soldiers became full-time professionals, rather than part-time militia.

Rump Parliament

The Rump Parliament is the name of the English Parliament after Colonel Pride purged the Long Parliament on 6 December 1648 of those members hostile to the Grandees' intention to try King Charles I for high treason.

'Rump' normally means the hind end of an animal; its use meaning 'remnant' was first recorded in the above context. Since 1649, the term 'rump parliament' has been used to refer to any parliament left over from the actual legitimate parliament.

Navigation Acts

The English Navigation Acts of 1712 were a series of laws that restricted the use of foreign shipping for trade between England (after 1707 Great Britain) and its colonies, a process which had started in 1651. Their goal was to force colonial development into lines favorable to England, and stop direct colonial trade with the Netherlands, France and other European countries.

The original ordinance of 1651 was renewed at the Restoration by Acts of 1660 and 1663, and subsequently subject to minor amendment. These Acts also formed the basis for British overseas trade for nearly 200 years.

David Hume

David Hume was a Scottish philosopher, historian, economist, and essayist, known especially for his philosophical empiricism and scepticism. He was one of the most important figures in the history of Western philosophy and the Scottish Enlightenment. Hume is often grouped with John Locke, George Berkeley, and a handful of others as a British Empiricist.

John Locke

John Locke, widely known as the Father of Liberalism, was an English philosopher and physician regarded as one of the most influential of Enlightenment thinkers. Considered one of the first of the British empiricists, following the tradition of Francis Bacon, he is equally important to social contract theory. His work had a great impact upon the development of epistemology and political philosophy.

Heinrich Heine

Heinrich Heine was one of the most significant German poets of the 19th century. He was also a journalist, essayist, and literary critic. He is best known outside Germany for his early lyric poetry, which was set to music in the form of Lieder (art songs) by composers such as Robert Schumann and Franz Schubert.

Dutch Republic

The Dutch Republic-officially known as the Republic of the Seven United Netherlands (Republiek der Zeven Verenigde Nederlanden), the Republic of the United Netherlands, or the Republic of the Seven United Provinces (Republiek der Zeven Verenigde Provinciën)-was a republic in Europe existing from 1581 to 1795, preceding the Batavian Republic, the United Kingdom of the Netherlands and ultimately the modern Kingdom of the Netherlands. Alternative names include the United Provinces (Verenigde Provinciën), Federated Dutch Provinces (Foederatae Belgii Provinciae), and Dutch Federation (Belgica Foederata).

Until the 16th century, the Low Countries-roughly now corresponding to Netherlands, Belgium and Luxembourg-consisted of a number of duchies, counties and bishoprics, most of which were under the supremacy of the Holy Roman Empire.

Golden Age

The term Golden Age comes from Greek mythology and legend and refers to the first in a sequence of four or five (or more) Ages of Man, in which the Golden Age is first, followed in sequence, by the Silver, Bronze, and Iron Ages, and then the present, a period of decline. By extension 'Golden Age' denotes a period of primordial peace, harmony, stability, and prosperity.

There are analogous concepts in the religious and philosophical traditions of the South Asian subcontinent.

1. The _________ was a civil war in France, occurring in the midst of the Franco-Spanish War, which had begun in 1635. The word _________ means sling, which Parisian mobs used to smash the windows of supporters of Cardinal Mazarin.

   The _________ was divided into two campaigns, the _________ of the parlements and the _________ of the nobles. The timing of the outbreak of the _________ des parlements, directly after the Peace of Westphalia (1648) that ended the Thirty Years War, was significant.

   a. Fronde
   b. Battle of the Faubourg St Antoine
   c. Cappel family
   d. Franco-Dutch War

2. The _________ was a period of cooling that occurred after the Medieval Warm Period (Medieval Climate Optimum). While it was not a true ice age, the term was introduced into the scientific literature by François E. Matthes in 1939. It has been conventionally defined as a period extending from the 16th to the 19th centuries, or alternatively, from about 1350 to about 1850, though climatologists and historians working with local records no longer expect to agree on either the start or end dates of this period, which varied according to local conditions. NASA defines the term as a cold period between AD 1550 and AD 1850 and notes three particularly cold intervals: one beginning about 1650, another about 1770, and the last in 1850, each separated by intervals of slight warming.

   a. Littorina Sea
   b. Little Ice Age
   c. Mesolithic
   d. Middle Bronze Age Cold Epoch

3. The _________, issued on April 13, 1598, by Henry IV of France, granted the Calvinist Protestants of France (also known as Huguenots) substantial rights in a nation still considered essentially Catholic. In the Edict Henry aimed primarily to promote civil unity. The Edict separated civil from religious unity, treated some Protestants for the first time as more than mere schismatics and heretics, and opened a path for secularism and tolerance.

   a. Edict of Versailles
   b. Edict of Nantes
   c. Second Servile War
   d. Coptic Catholic Church

4. The _________ was the lower house of the National Assembly of the Republic of Korea during its Second Republic. The _________ was established by the Constitution of the Second Republic of Korea, which established a bicameral legislature.

   a. Congress of Deputies
   b. House of Representatives
   c. House of Commons
   d. Second Servile War

5. _________s occur if there is shortage of food and/or unequal distribution of food. Causes can be harvest failures, incompetent food storage, transport problems, food speculation, hoarding, poisoning of food, or attacks by pests like locusts. When the public becomes too desperate in such conditions, they may attack shops, farms, homes, or government buildings to attain bread or other staple foods like grain or salt, as in the 1977 Egyptian Bread Riots .

   a. Flour Riot of 1837
   b. Food riot
   c. Merthyr Rising
   d. Novgorod Uprising of 1650

Visit Cram101.com for full Practice Exams

ANSWER KEY
16. Absolutism and Constitutionalism in Europe, ca. 1589-1725

1. a
2. b
3. b
4. c
5. b

You can take the complete Chapter Practice Test

for 16. Absolutism and Constitutionalism in Europe, ca. 1589-1725
on all key terms, persons, places, and concepts.

Online 99 Cents

http://www.epub141.56.21995.16.cram101.com/

Use www.Cram101.com for all your study needs

including Cram101's online interactive problem solving labs in

chemistry, statistics, mathematics, and more.

17. Toward a New Worldview, 1540-1789

CHAPTER OUTLINE: KEY TERMS, PEOPLE, PLACES, CONCEPTS

Scientific revolution

Thomas Aquinas

Alchemy

Galileo Galilei

Isaac Newton

Francis Bacon

Andreas Vesalius

Robert Boyle

Mary Astell

Protestantism

Society

Counter-Reformation

Enlightenment

Gaius Marius

Baruch Spinoza

Pierre Bayle

Christian worldview

Jewish thought

John Locke

Tabula rasa

International trade

17. Toward a New Worldview, 1540-1789

CHAPTER OUTLINE: KEY TERMS, PEOPLE, PLACES, CONCEPTS

______	David Hume
______	Immanuel Kant
______	Jean-Jacques Rousseau
______	Rococo
______	James Beattie
______	Frederick the Great
______	Prussia
______	Seven Years' War
______	War of the Austrian Succession

CHAPTER HIGHLIGHTS & NOTES: KEY TERMS, PEOPLE, PLACES, CONCEPTS

Scientific revolution	The scientific revolution is an era associated primarily with the 16th and 17th centuries during which new ideas and knowledge in physics, astronomy, biology, medicine and chemistry transformed medieval and ancient views of nature and laid the foundations for modern science. According to most accounts, the scientific revolution began in Europe towards the end of the Renaissance era and continued through the late 18th century, the later period known as The Enlightenment. It was sparked by the publication in 1543 of two works that changed the course of science: Nicolaus Copernicus's De revolutionibus orbium coelestium (On the Revolutions of the Heavenly Spheres) and Andreas Vesalius's De humani corporis fabrica (On the Fabric of the Human body).
Thomas Aquinas	Thomas Aquinas, O.P. , also Thomas of Aquin or Aquino, was an Italian Dominican priest of the Roman Catholic Church, and an immensely influential philosopher and theologian in the tradition of scholasticism, known as Doctor Angelicus ([the] Angelic Doctor), Doctor Communis, or Doctor Universalis. 'Aquinas' is not a surname, but is a Latin demonym for a resident of Aquino, his place of birth. He was the foremost classical proponent of natural theology, and the father of Thomism.

Visit Cram101.com for full Practice Exams

Alchemy	Alchemy is an ancient tradition, the primary objective of which was the creation of a fabled elixir, known as the Philosopher's Stone, capable of turning any base metal into gold or silver, the same also acting as a universal medicine said to indefinitely prolong youth and keep one from death. The alchemists themselves stressed that the operation was natural, being a microcosm of the world itself, and following the same principles of development that apply to plants, animals and minerals. Today it is widely believed that the alchemical processes were allegorical as metaphors for a spiritual discipline, akin to a technique for the obtainment of enlightenment.
Galileo Galilei	Galileo Galilei, commonly known as Galileo, was an Italian physicist, mathematician, astronomer and philosopher who played a major role in the Scientific Revolution. His achievements include improvements to the telescope and consequent astronomical observations, and support for Copernicanism. Galileo has been called the 'father of modern observational astronomy', the 'father of modern physics', the 'father of science', and 'the Father of Modern Science'.
Isaac Newton	Sir Isaac Newton PRS MP (25 December 1642 - 20 March 1727 [NS: 4 January 1643 - 31 March 1727]) was an English physicist, mathematician, astronomer, natural philosopher, alchemist, and theologian, who has been 'considered by many to be the greatest and most influential scientist who ever lived.' His monograph Philosophiæ Naturalis Principia Mathematica, published in 1687, lays the foundations for most of classical mechanics. In this work, Newton described universal gravitation and the three laws of motion, which dominated the scientific view of the physical universe for the next three centuries. Newton showed that the motions of objects on Earth and of celestial bodies are governed by the same set of natural laws, by demonstrating the consistency between Kepler's laws of planetary motion and his theory of gravitation, thus removing the last doubts about heliocentrism and advancing the Scientific Revolution.
Francis Bacon	Francis Bacon, 1st Viscount St Alban(s), KC (22 January 1561 - 9 April 1626) was an English philosopher, statesman, scientist, jurist and author. He served both as Attorney General and Lord Chancellor of England. Although his political career ended in disgrace, he remained extremely influential through his works, especially as philosophical advocate and practitioner of the scientific method during the scientific revolution.
Andreas Vesalius	Andreas Vesalius was an anatomist, physician, and author of one of the most influential books on human anatomy, De humani corporis fabrica (On the Fabric of the Human Body). Vesalius is often referred to as the founder of modern human anatomy. Vesalius is the Latinized form of Andreas van Wesel.
Robert Boyle	Robert Boyle, FRS, (25 January 1627 - 31 December 1691) was a 17th-century natural philosopher, chemist, physicist, and inventor, also noted for his writings in theology. He has been variously described as Irish, English and Anglo-Irish, his father having come to Ireland from England during the time of the Plantations.

Visit Cram101.com for full Practice Exams

17. Toward a New Worldview, 1540-1789

Mary Astell

Mary Astell was an English feminist writer and rhetorician. Her advocacy of equal educational opportunities for women has earned her the title 'the first English feminist.'

Life and career

Few records of Mary Astell's life have survived. As biographer Ruth Perry explains, 'as a woman she had little or no business in the world of commerce, politics, or law.

Protestantism

Protestantism is one of the major groupings within Christianity. It has been defined as 'any of several church denominations denying the universal authority of the Pope and affirming the Reformation principles of justification by faith alone, the priesthood of all believers, and the primacy of the Bible as the only source of revealed truth' and, more broadly, to mean Christianity outside 'of a Catholic or Eastern church'. It is a movement that began in Germany in the early 16th century as a reaction against medieval Roman Catholic doctrines and practices, especially in regards to salvation, justification, and ecclesiology.

Society

A society, is a group of people related to each other through persistent relations, or a large social grouping sharing the same geographical or virtual territory, subject to the same political authority and dominant cultural expectations. Human societies are characterized by patterns of relationships (social relations) between individuals who share a distinctive culture and institutions; a given society may be described as the sum total of such relationships among its constituent members. In the social sciences, a larger society often evinces stratification and/or dominance patterns in subgroups.

Counter-Reformation

The Counter-Reformation was the period of Catholic revival beginning with the Council of Trent (1545-1563) and ending at the close of the Thirty Years' War (1648), which is sometimes considered a response to the Protestant Reformation. The Counter-Reformation was a comprehensive effort composed of four major elements:•Ecclesiastical or structural reconfiguration•Religious orders•Spiritual movements•Political dimensions

Such reforms included the foundation of seminaries for the proper training of priests in the spiritual life and the theological traditions of the Church, the reform of religious life by returning orders to their spiritual foundations, and new spiritual movements focusing on the devotional life and a personal relationship with Christ, including the Spanish mystics and the French school of spirituality. It also involved political activities that included the Roman Inquisition.

Enlightenment

Enlightenment in a secular context often means the 'full comprehension of a situation', but in spiritual terms the word alludes to a spiritual revelation or deep insight into the meaning and purpose of all things, communication with or understanding of the mind of God, profound spiritual understanding or a fundamentally changed consciousness whereby everything is perceived as a unity.

Some scientists believe that during meditative states leading up to the subjective experience of enlightenment there are actual physical changes in the brain. Buddhism

The English term 'enlightenment' has commonly been used to translate several Sanskrit, Pali, Chinese and Japanese terms and concepts, especially bodhi, prajna, kensho, satori and buddhahood.

Gaius Marius

Gaius Marius was a Roman general and statesman. He was elected consul an unprecedented seven times during his career. He was also noted for his dramatic reforms of Roman armies, authorizing recruitment of landless citizens, eliminating the manipular military formations, and reorganizing the structure of the legions into separate cohorts. His life and career were significant in Rome's transformation from Republic to Empire.

Baruch Spinoza

Baruch Spinoza and later Benedict de Spinoza (24 November 1632 - 21 February 1677) was a Dutch philosopher. Revealing considerable scientific aptitude, the breadth and importance of Spinoza's work was not fully realized until years after his death. By laying the groundwork for the 18th century Enlightenment and modern biblical criticism, he came to be considered one of the great rationalists of 17th-century philosophy.

Pierre Bayle

Pierre Bayle was a French philosopher and writer best known for his seminal work the Historical and Critical Dictionary, published beginning in 1695.

Bayle was a self-pronounced Protestant, and as a fideist he advocated a separation between the spheres of faith and reason, on the grounds of God being incomprehensible to man. As a forerunner of the Encyclopedists and an advocate of the principle of the toleration of divergent beliefs, his works subsequently influenced the development of the Enlightenment.

Christian worldview

Christian worldview refers to the framework of ideas and beliefs through which a Christian individual, group or culture interprets the world and interacts with it. Different denominations of Christianity have varying worldviews. There are varieties of particulars within the Christian worldview, and disputes of the meaning of concepts in a Christian worldview, but certain thematic elements are common in the Christian worldview.

Jewish thought

Jewish Thought is a field of Jewish Studies that deals with the products of Jewish thought and culture throughout the ages, and their historical development. The field also deals with the connections, parallels, and influences, between Jewish ways of thought and world philosophy in general.

The term 'Jewish Thought' was originally suggested by Rabbi Abraham Isaac Kook, within the framework of the founding of his central Israeli Yeshiva, Mercaz HaRav.

Visit Cram101.com for full Practice Exams

17. Toward a New Worldview, 1540-1789

CHAPTER HIGHLIGHTS & NOTES: KEY TERMS, PEOPLE, PLACES, CONCEPTS

John Locke	John Locke, widely known as the Father of Liberalism, was an English philosopher and physician regarded as one of the most influential of Enlightenment thinkers. Considered one of the first of the British empiricists, following the tradition of Francis Bacon, he is equally important to social contract theory. His work had a great impact upon the development of epistemology and political philosophy.
Tabula rasa	Tabula rasa is the epistemological theory that individuals are born without built-in mental content and that their knowledge comes from experience and perception. Generally proponents of the tabula rasa thesis favour the 'nurture' side of the nature versus nurture debate, when it comes to aspects of one's personality, social and emotional behaviour, and intelligence. The term in Latin equates to the English 'blank slate' (or more accurately, 'erased slate') (which refers to writing on a slate sheet in chalk) but comes from the Roman tabula or wax tablet, used for notes, which was blanked by heating the wax and then smoothing it to give a tabula rasa.
International trade	International trade is the exchange of capital, goods, and services across international borders or territories. In most countries, such trade represents a significant share of gross domestic product (GDP). While international trade has been present throughout much of history, its economic, social, and political importance has been on the rise in recent centuries.
David Hume	David Hume was a Scottish philosopher, historian, economist, and essayist, known especially for his philosophical empiricism and scepticism. He was one of the most important figures in the history of Western philosophy and the Scottish Enlightenment. Hume is often grouped with John Locke, George Berkeley, and a handful of others as a British Empiricist.
Immanuel Kant	Immanuel Kant was a German philosopher from Königsberg, who researched, lectured, and wrote on philosophy and anthropology during the Enlightenment at the end of the 18th century. At the time, there were major successes and advances in the sciences (for example, Isaac Newton, Carl Friedrich Gauss, and Robert Boyle) applying reason and logic. Kant's major work, the Critique of Pure Reason (Kritik der reinen Vernunft, 1781), aimed to unite reason with experience to move beyond what he took to be failures of traditional philosophy and metaphysics.
Jean-Jacques Rousseau	Jean-Jacques Rousseau was a Genevan philosopher, writer, and composer of 18th-century Romanticism of French expression. His political philosophy influenced the French Revolution as well as the overall development of modern political, sociological, and educational thought. Jean-Jacques Rousseau's novel Émile: or, On Education is a treatise on the education of the whole person for citizenship.

Visit Cram101.com for full Practice Exams

Rococo	Rococo less commonly roccoco, also referred to as 'Late Baroque', is an 18th-century artistic movement and style, which affected several aspects of the arts including painting, sculpture, architecture, interior design, decoration, literature, music and theatre. The Rococo developed in the early part of the 18th century in Paris, France as a reaction against the grandeur, symmetry and strict regulations of the Baroque, especially that of the Palace of Versailles. In such a way, Rococo artists opted for a more jocular, florid and graceful approach to Baroque art and architecture.
James Beattie	Professor James Beattie FRSE (25 October 1735 - 18 August 1803) was a Scottish poet, moralist and philosopher. He was born the son of a shopkeeper and small farmer at Laurencekirk in the Mearns, and educated at Aberdeen University. In 1760, he was appointed Professor of moral philosophy there as a result of the interest of his intimate friend, Robert Arbuthnot of Haddo.
Frederick the Great	Frederick II was a King in Prussia (1740-1772) and a King of Prussia (1772-1786) from the Hohenzollern dynasty. In his role as a prince-elector of the Holy Roman Empire, he was also Elector of Brandenburg. He was in personal union the sovereign prince of the Principality of Neuchâtel. He became known as Frederick the Great and was nicknamed Der Alte Fritz ('Old Fritz').
Prussia	Prussia is a historical region in Central Europe extending from the south-eastern coast of the Baltic Sea to the Masurian Lake District. It is now divided between Poland, Russia, and Lithuania. The former German state of Prussia derived its name from the region.
Seven Years' War	The Seven Years' War was a global military conflict between 1756 and 1763, involving most of the great powers of the time affecting North and Central America, Europe, the West African coast, India and the Philippines. espective theaters: French and Indian War (North America, 1754-1763), Pomeranian War (Sweden, 1757-1762), Third Carnatic War (India, 1757-1763) and Third Silesian War . The war was driven by the antagonism between Great Britain (in personal union with Hanover) and the Bourbons (in France and Spain), resulting from overlapping interests in their colonial and trade empires, and by the antagonism between the Hohenzollerns and Habsburgs (Holy Roman Emperors and archdukes in Austria), resulting from territorial and hegemonial conflicts in the Holy Roman Empire.
War of the Austrian Succession	The War of the Austrian Succession - also known as King George's War in North America, and incorporating the War of Jenkins' Ear with Spain and two of the three Silesian wars - involved nearly all the powers of Europe, except for the Polish-Lithuanian Commonwealth, the Portuguese Empire and the Ottoman Empire.

Visit Cram101.com for full Practice Exams

17. Toward a New Worldview, 1540-1789

CHAPTER HIGHLIGHTS & NOTES: KEY TERMS, PEOPLE, PLACES, CONCEPTS

The war began under the pretext that Maria Theresa of Austria was ineligible to succeed to the Habsburg thrones of her father, Charles VI, because Salic law precluded royal inheritance by a woman, though in reality this was a convenient excuse put forward by Prussia and France to challenge Habsburg power. Austria was supported by Great Britain and the Dutch Republic, the traditional enemies of France, as well as the Kingdom of Sardinia and Saxony.

CHAPTER QUIZ: KEY TERMS, PEOPLE, PLACES, CONCEPTS

1. The _________ is an era associated primarily with the 16th and 17th centuries during which new ideas and knowledge in physics, astronomy, biology, medicine and chemistry transformed medieval and ancient views of nature and laid the foundations for modern science. According to most accounts, the _________ began in Europe towards the end of the Renaissance era and continued through the late 18th century, the later period known as The Enlightenment. It was sparked by the publication in 1543 of two works that changed the course of science: Nicolaus Copernicus's De revolutionibus orbium coelestium (On the Revolutions of the Heavenly Spheres) and Andreas Vesalius's De humani corporis fabrica (On the Fabric of the Human body).

   a. Second Green Revolution
   b. Twitter Revolution
   c. Scientific revolution
   d. Baptism of Poland

2. _________, O.P. , also Thomas of Aquin or Aquino, was an Italian Dominican priest of the Roman Catholic Church, and an immensely influential philosopher and theologian in the tradition of scholasticism, known as Doctor Angelicus ([the] Angelic Doctor), Doctor Communis, or Doctor Universalis. 'Aquinas' is not a surname, but is a Latin demonym for a resident of Aquino, his place of birth. He was the foremost classical proponent of natural theology, and the father of Thomism.

   a. Thomas Aquinas
   b. Waldensians
   c. Second Servile War
   d. Baptism of Poland

3. . _________, FRS, (25 January 1627 - 31 December 1691) was a 17th-century natural philosopher, chemist, physicist, and inventor, also noted for his writings in theology. He has been variously described as Irish, English and Anglo-Irish, his father having come to Ireland from England during the time of the Plantations.

   Although his research clearly has its roots in the alchemical tradition, Boyle is largely regarded today as the first modern chemist, and therefore one of the founders of modern chemistry, and one of the pioneers of modern experimental scientific method.

a. Giordano Bruno
b. Robert Boyle
c. Joseph Butler
d. Samuel Clarke

4. _________ is an ancient tradition, the primary objective of which was the creation of a fabled elixir, known as the Philosopher's Stone, capable of turning any base metal into gold or silver, the same also acting as a universal medicine said to indefinitely prolong youth and keep one from death. The alchemists themselves stressed that the operation was natural, being a microcosm of the world itself, and following the same principles of development that apply to plants, animals and minerals. Today it is widely believed that the alchemical processes were allegorical as metaphors for a spiritual discipline, akin to a technique for the obtainment of enlightenment.

a. arsenal
b. Alchemy
c. Economic Stimulus Act of 2008
d. Investiture Controversy

5. _________, 1st Viscount St Alban(s), KC (22 January 1561 - 9 April 1626) was an English philosopher, statesman, scientist, jurist and author. He served both as Attorney General and Lord Chancellor of England. Although his political career ended in disgrace, he remained extremely influential through his works, especially as philosophical advocate and practitioner of the scientific method during the scientific revolution.

a. Pierre Bayle
b. Balthasar Bekker
c. George Berkeley
d. Francis Bacon

Visit Cram101.com for full Practice Exams

ANSWER KEY
17. Toward a New Worldview, 1540-1789

---

1. c

2. a

3. b

4. b

5. d

You can take the complete Chapter Practice Test

for 17. Toward a New Worldview, 1540-1789
on all key terms, persons, places, and concepts.

Online 99 Cents

http://www.epub141.56.21995.17.cram101.com/

Use www.Cram101.com for all your study needs

including Cram101's online interactive problem solving labs in

chemistry, statistics, mathematics, and more.

Want More?
Cram101.com...

Cram101.com provides the outlines and highlights of your textbooks, just like this e-StudyGuide, but also gives you the PRACTICE TESTS, and other exclusive study tools for all of your textbooks.

Learn More. ***Just click***
http://www.cram101.com/

Other Cram101 e-Books and Tests

CPSIA information can be obtained at www.ICGtesting.com
Printed in the USA
LVOW09s1026100913

351791LV00001B/8/P

9 781478 493334